Philanthropy & Sport

A Real Game Changer

LYN WATNER

To: The best Mom ever, who could told me a 100 time "I told you so" + never once did she say it. with love, respect + devotion.

Editing Monica Guetre
Published by Emerald Publications
Printed in Canada

ISBN-10 - 1502415615
ISBN-13-978-1502415615

DEDICATION

This book is dedicated to my parents
Hya and Edward Heine and Eddie Murray.

My parents gave me the encouragement and advice to follow my heart and start my own business. They were both believers in what I could accomplish. I am only sorry my Dad was not here when I started LMW Non Profit Associates. They let me be the turtle who sticks her neck out.

Eddie Murray is my dearest friend who not only taught me about baseball, he also gave me inspiration to write this book. He has been a great friend and confidant over the years and I am blessed to have him in my life.

ACKNOWLEDGMENTS

I want to thank Nadine Nicholson and the great women I met in my Freedom Focus class who encouraged me to take on this endeavor by giving me support during the four months it took me to write this book. Nadine, my coach, had the foresight to suggest that I needed a different platform to give my business a 'kick start'. When she mentioned that I should write a book, at first I was mortified. Then I met Les Kletke and he has been a fantastic writing coach! I have enjoyed every minute writing this book. I want to thank each of the athletes, Eddie Murray, Jimmy Jones, Pam Shiver, Rick Dempsey, Andrea Seefeldt Knight and Scott McGregor for giving their time to share their stories with me.

CONTENTS

CHAPTER 1

WHY NOW?

Growing up on a horse farm was the best way to learn about nature, the power of the outdoors and knowing that your life would always be full of adventures. And mine has been! Riding a horse whenever I wanted, learning all the trails so that I could go out alone and commune with nature was like living in a dream. I loved being a tomboy and at an early age learned to do everything that my older brother did. Thoughts of being in the kitchen were not for me instead I played sports, field hockey, tennis, volleyball and any other outdoor activity that kept me away from the house.

I grew up Jewish, although the community I lived in was mostly non-Jewish with a level of tolerance that never really invaded my space. One thing about being Jewish was that from a very early age I learned that giving back to your community was and still is a tremendous obligation. While attending Sunday school we learned about Tzedakah (charity) and Tikkun Olam (making the world a better place).

As a young student in Sunday school, every class had to do a charitable activity and my class always visited the elderly in a nursing home. Not everyone was Jewish; in fact, it was quite diverse. Visiting the elderly was my first introduction to giving back! It also taught me that giving back was for all people needing help. Charity or making the world a better place has always crossed cultural and ethnic lines. People like Mother Teresa, Martin Luther King, Princess Diana, Florence Nightingale, Gandhi, Albert Schweitzer, George Clooney and Angelina Jolie have all made a difference in the world and in their communities. They ignore differences in ethnicity and religion putting themselves secondary to their mission. These two concepts, charity and saving the world, became the main reason why I ultimately became a professional fundraiser.

Anyone can give back to their community or to someone in need. By becoming involved with people or organizations that need volunteers this creates a new vision of who you are and what you stand for. It's easy to say that you can't help. You do have your own issues to get in order and you may think that you have nothing to offer, when the reality is once, you get up off the couch and get out there; you will be surprised at how much you do have to offer. Do it today, yesterday is gone and who knows what tomorrow will bring.

Why do I think now is the time? I am in my early 60s and believe that I still have a great many opportunities to make my community a better place. With more than 1.5 million non-profits just in the United States alone, giving back can make a huge difference in many communities and it can motivate individuals to help the less fortunate. Non-profits need volunteers for diverse jobs such as giving blood, answering phones, assisting with bookkeeping, handing out meals to the elderly, teaching, reading, tutoring and mentoring and the list goes on.

In today's economy, there is even a greater need for volunteers. Many unemployed people have talents that could be put to good use in helping others. Just because you don't have, a job doesn't mean you can't be productive in today's society. Sometimes it is just too easy to take a back seat and feel sorry for yourself. Everyone has something to offer their community to make it a better place. Besides, you never know when a volunteer job may take a right turn and become a full time job.

I have always fallen into a volunteer niche because I fight for the underdog. I met the Executive Director of Child First Authority a non-profit that creates after-school programs for 21 inner city schools in Baltimore, Maryland. They had no fundraiser on staff and needed assistance to raise money for existing and new programs. At first, I joined their development committee. My role changed after the initial introduction to the programs because of the enthusiasm that bubbled up from the students. I was asked to sit on the Board then, about 18 months later during a board retreat I became the President of the Board. This can happen to anyone who wants to be engaged, even if they are out of work or feel inclined to help a nonprofit advance their work with your talent.

I was taught at an early age to be a leader and not a follower and that advice has put me to where I am today. The truth be known, everyone - leaders or followers - have a skill that can be offered to help individuals or non-profits. You don't have to be shy about your capabilities, whether it is teaching, creating or assisting someone else with their sense of a 'Can Do' philosophy. Everyone has a skill that someone else does not have and that someone else may need to learn a new skill to better prepare themselves for a new life or a new job.

Three things can make a difference to any organization or non-profit, time, money and expertise. If you have time, volunteer, if you have money, be generous and if you have expertise, share your talents with someone else who needs to learn a new skill. It is difficult enough not having a job, yet it is so much more meaningful if you help others by teaching what you already know. Everyone has resources and even if you may think these are insignificant, they really aren't. If you share your experiences with someone less fortunate, you are doing a great service to that person as well as feeling good about helping someone else.

So many people today, who feel lost, believe that they have no passion within themselves to help others and don't realize their passion for sharing is lying dormant. Sitting on a couch all day and feeling sorry for yourself, does not bring value to you or anyone else. I strongly believe that everyone has passion for giving back to someone and their community. Many people just do not take the time to delve inside themselves and search for what they are passionate about. When you explore your own passion this also draws out the same actions in others or leads to another way of giving back. By volunteering, you can bring value to your own life. By helping others not only find their passion, it creates avenues of interest for everyone. Giving back is less about money and more about what is inside you.

Everyone has skills that are transferable. Do not listen to the inner voice that says, "No one cares about my skills," so that you end up staying on the couch. In an economy that is struggling to make a comeback, it requires everyone to stand up, be exactly who you are and show what you have to offer. There will be people who won't want what you offer however, by telling your own story on how you discovered your true passion you can help others find their true passion. Skills and expertise cover a multitude of areas in cooking, carpentry, exercise, hiking, biking, electrical skills, plumbing, mechanics, painter, artist and writer and on and on. I am sure that many people down on their luck feel that giving back is a waste of time I assure you it isn't. There is an adrenaline rush when you help someone learn a new skill set or when they just find their own passion. This in itself is a huge thrill.

I am sure many of you think that rich people just give back because they can. Creating an aura of philanthropy means many things to many people. Everyone's motives are different. Your personal motivation may be putting your name on a building, making a contribution that will save lives, believing it is a rite of passage to have enough money to give away, making an anonymous contribution, donating gifts in-kind such as something tangible like a piece of art, furniture, real estate, a car or even a kidney because you think it will get you to heaven and the list does go on. By creating all these opportunities, an easy case is made that giving back is important.

Really rich people often start foundations that require them to donate a percentage, which is usually 5% of the foundation's income directed towards non-profits. Ultimately, giving back (Tzedakah) gives you a feeling of satisfaction when someone else's life becomes better and productive. Finding your passion can be fun, creative and very rewarding. You want your passion to light and lift you up as well, so that you can be productive while helping others.

Of course, to do this, you must want to get up off the couch and take action! If you don't know your passion, start a list of possible areas that might give you a real buzz, tantalize your nerve endings and get you really excited. You might even be inclined to share your passion with a close friend who also realizes they too would like to find their passion. It is easier to help someone else when you are on the path to creating something new for yourself.

There are many ways to search for your passion. The most obvious is the Internet! No surprise since there is a multitude of national non-profits in the United States as well as many in each state, city, county and municipality. Search for non-profits by category such as education, higher education, academics, after school programs, sports, chess, debates, athletics, gardening, driver training, painting, making jewelry, walking dogs, assisting a vet and many more. Go to the library and just peruse the stacks; it may very well inspire you to find your passion.

Upon finding your passion and if you are serious about assisting others in their search, give them advice on how to navigate the Internet and describe how you found your own passion.

Some other ideas that help in the search for your passion can be in newspapers or listening to national public radio station members such as NPR or WYPR in your area. Non-profits often advertise on public radio stations that in turn lets you know about their mission. Check out public bulletin boards in the library, Starbucks, Panera's, schools, hairdressers, food stores and community centers. In addition, many libraries have magazine and newspaper stacks with information on or for non-profits that might be mission driven. Ask for some pointers from your clergy, teachers, friends, colleagues and people you know who already work for a non-profit.

Many organizations are looking for mentors and volunteers for different events or activities or sometimes a new skill that can be taught to others. Red Cross always needs blood donations, Big Brothers and Big Sisters search for mentors, the YMCA or the YWCA always need volunteers to assist with a variety of programs. In the summer, sports organizations and teams are looking for lifeguards, coaches and instructors. During the school year, teachers are looking for volunteers or tutors, assistance in class organization and activities. What about volunteering with the Girl Scouts and Boys Scouts? The SPCA also needs volunteers to help them with the animals.

This chapter is called 'Why Now?' By getting involved today, you can make a commitment to yourself and your desire to create a better community. Getting off the couch to be a coach or a mentor will make you feel like you have turned your life around and make it easier for the next person to do the same. You can be a leader instead of a follower! You will see that by taking one-step it will lead you to a better life and could easily include a new job!

CHAPTER 2

THE BUSINESS OF BASEBALL

As I may have mentioned, I was a tomboy growing up. Mostly it was clear to me that my father's expectations were that I should and could do everything my brother did. Living on a horse farm with mastiffs and a basset hound that accompanied my Dad, my brother and me while riding the trails, was a great way to grow up. I always felt connected to my horse. There was a sense of wellbeing riding those trails whenever I wanted.

Riding with my brother was always a challenge. If he rode behind me, he'd throw rocks at the rump of my horse causing her to constantly kick her back feet out. If he rode in front of me, he would hold a branch just long enough so that when my horse and I passed, the branch would either hit my horse's face or mine. The freedom of the outdoors was always invigorating and gave me the opportunity to be myself and learn independence.

When I grew older, I consciously wondered what I would do as an adult. I always thought adult women, became teachers, got married and had children. At least that was what I thought women did.

In 1971, I took my junior college year abroad in Mexico City, Mexico and ended up living in Mexico for six years. I had some great experiences and accomplished much while living there. After living there for just two years, people started asking me what part of Latin

America was I from because my Spanish was so good that I no longer had an accent. That was a huge personal accomplishment.

When I returned to my hometown, Baltimore, Maryland in 1976, I was bilingual and had a B.A. in International Relations with an emphasis on Latin American Affairs. I needed a job and lucky for me I knew a lawyer, Ron Shapiro who had worked with my Dad before he died. Ron first suggested that I should work on a political campaign for one of the Democrats running for Governor. That gig lasted about 3 months and then I was on the street again. It was my first look at local politics and it was clear to me that the women attempting to run a campaign were clueless.

I needed another job and Ron had recently started a sports management company with Brooks Robinson, the recently retired 3rd baseman for the Orioles. Ron managed about 4 or 5 players at that time and had just signed Dennis Martinez, a pitcher from Nicaragua as the newest client. Dennis spoke some English and his wife spoke very little. Ron asked if I would help Dennis get acclimated with a house, help with a school for the kids, find doctors, show them how to get around from place to place and help with whatever else was needed. It seemed like a great beginning, starting with a new company, being bilingual and I knew that whatever I decided to do, I would do well. I knew that I could do anything! Ron had asked if I would just help out for three weeks. Instead of weeks, I was there for almost 10 years.

Was I concerned that I had no background in sports, other than playing sports as a child and young adult? No. I do have to say though, that I came from of a family that dabbled in a variety of sports. I had a great-uncle who was Commissioner of Horse Racing, a grandfather who owned the Baltimore Colts until the early 50s and my Dad had worked with a group of men from Baltimore to bring the original Bullets, basketball team, to Baltimore. I loved horseracing and I had a dream that one day I would ride in the women's only horse race, the Powder Puff Derby that was held before the Preakness. I never did get to ride in the Derby. I knew that many of my life experiences would make this job easier for me. Having lived in a foreign country, I learned the skill of adapting and blending in quickly. I also knew that when I exposed myself to new experiences, I always walked away with a lesson learned. Besides, having been taught that I could do anything my brother did, I knew this was going to be a great job!

Honestly, there was never a moment that I thought I was working in a chauvinist environment. Honestly, I never really thought much about the game of baseball, because I thought baseball was boring. In fact, I would go to the games and read. One of our clients, Eddie Murray would hold his hands up in front of his face, mimicking me as if he was reading as well.

I worked in Ron's law office for the first three to four years and then we moved an office uptown. When we moved there were only three employees, so I did the bookkeeping, paid the bills and handled any and all issues when the players needed assistance. I was the infamous 'Gal Friday'. As we hired staff, a lawyer, an accountant and the administrator, we moved once again, this time to the suburbs. Being the 'Gal Friday' never seemed demeaning to me. In fact, I had a nickname that Eddie Murray had given to me, 'The Hatch Lady'. Why? Because I took care of everything and did it, right the first time.

For me, I was there to do the best for each of my clients and to tell them the truth about the length of time they would spend at any promotional event, what they really needed to do to save more money or just listen to complaints about the game itself. I did wake up-calls, made sure that special requests were fulfilled such as a having an extra hard mattress for a player at spring training. I was available for anything that needed to be accomplished, spoke to their mothers and their wives and kept every secret no matter how little or how large. I even went through rehab with two different players, once for a DWI and once with another player caught for drug possession. Rehab was not always fun for me but I was able to give the players the reassurance they needed to get through the four weeks of a difficult situation. I'd get calls in the middle of night about the lousy call the umpire made at a game, or from a player wanting to buy a new suit but had no money, another player who wanted a third car and he wasn't even married.

The task that I had most fun with besides being there for the players was negotiating the winter ball contracts for the young guys who were going to South America, Mexico, Central America and the Dominican Republic. In the beginning, our lawyers and the foreign

General Managers (GM) wanted to negotiate with each other. It quickly became clear that there was a major language barrier. At first when I spoke to these GMs, they were skeptical about what I knew about the game. There was a scout from Mexico who was willing to negotiate with me and bam! Right after that, they all realized that not only did I speak great Spanish I also understood baseball.

I realized that I was not making as much money as the men in the office and even when I earned two Master's degrees from Johns Hopkins University, one in Administrative Sciences, which, in the 80s was the equivalent to an MBA; it really did not seem to affect my salary. Despite their dismissive attitude, towards me, it felt great to have accomplished so much. While working, I never really thought about the 'glass ceiling' until Sports Illustrated and the Baltimore Sun wrote articles about me pointing out that I was the only woman Sports Agent in Major League Baseball.

When I look back now, I had no fear. I knew that even if some mistakes were made, as long as the players respected me and knew that I was doing the best for them this was all that mattered. I was confident and perhaps even believed at times that no one could do a better job than I did. With confidence, came acceptance from many of the other players that we represented and the acceptance of many of the GMs as well. In those early years, most agents were men and when they finally acknowledged that I was more than just a secretary, I knew I was accepted. Actually, the attitude was rather comical, because I was a stockholder in the company and a Vice President. Really, what meant the most to me was being there for the players.

I knew that starting a job where I was in the minority, I would have slip ups and falls, still I also knew that I would always pick myself up, move forward and learn a lesson from each 'mishap'. I have always lived a life with no regrets because I always learned a lesson from those 'mishaps'. I learned that holding my head up, looking people in the eye and speaking my mind even when my Spanish grammar was wrong, showed that I was confident. Women can do anything that men can do. Moreover, if you make a mistake, learn from it and realize what is the worst that can happen, you fall, pick yourself up and acknowledge the lesson learned!

Today, women have made great strides in moving closer to the 'glass ceiling' and I still get calls from young women and men who want to know how to break into the sports business today. I tell them its different now than it was back in the 80s, but if you are confident, if you are not afraid to break through the barriers, you can be a great asset to your clients.

Just recently, I received a call from a young woman who wants to help retired players make a difference after baseball. She had tried calling the individual teams and was getting nowhere. When she called me, we did some internet searching and realized that there were several women in the Major League Baseball Association that might be able to help her. She is moving forward with caution and yet is confident she will get the job done.

It is clear life is not always, what you think it will be. I was never a teacher, and I did marry but never had natural born children of my own. I have been fortunate enough to have three careers and recently I have started my own consulting firm working with non-profits. Your life is what you make it and the twist and turns it takes will only make it more exciting.

CHAPTER 3

WHY SPORTS AND PHILANTHROPY

Philanthropy has become the number one indicator of how to improve a community. By assisting, a non-profit to reach their fundraising objectives this in turn gives the investor the opportunity to feel and see they are making a difference.

Philanthropists are individuals who give to Red Cross blood drives a few times a year, a person who volunteers at a senior center or day care program or a teenager who goes to the elder care facility and talks to the patients. She is also the woman who brings a pet to see sick children or the infirmed in a hospital providing a distraction or the man who feels he needs to give to the homeless because they are down on their luck. Philanthropy has many faces and it is not always about dollars given, it is about acts of kindness that will give someone less fortunate, hope.

There are seven faces of philanthropy: community activists, the devout, the investor, the socialite, the humanitarian focused on social causes, the benefactor who just wants to give back because it is the right thing to do and the affluent who pass money on to the next generation. Let's take a look at why each group believes that philanthropy or giving back is important.

The community activist gives because their sense of belonging comes from enhancing the services provided by non-profits, which enrich the lives of their constituents. It is important to keep in mind, that each community has its own history and culture that individuals want to preserve and augment through each generation.

The devout believe that philanthropy is the will of God and have a strong moral obligation to take responsibility for creating a better world. Many in this group do not seek recognition for volunteering for their time, money or talent.

The investor is just that. They see philanthropy as a good investment. Their motivation is purely about personal taxes, estate benefits and their own wealth. This group pursues non-profits and organizations that are more 'business-like' and effectively responds to private initiatives.

The socialites are out to have fun, do good work and give money. Their motivation is to have bigger and more costly events compared to the previous event. These events are about socializing and entertainment as well as how much money their event can raise!

The humanitarians focus on giving to social causes that fulfill their own sense of purpose. This group believes giving a contribution is a moral imperative and should be the responsibility of everyone.

Benefactors give back because they are grateful for medical or educational benefits they have received. One of their concerns is to give to organizations that are conscious of their fiscal responsibilities so they can focus on their client's needs.

The affluent focus on their family wealth and they have a strong desire that each successive generation increases their wealth as well as concentrating on the self-concept of philanthropy. Giving for them is a positive self-identity that strengthens family values making philanthropy the responsibility of everyone.

Now that we know there are 'Seven Faces' of philanthropy, how does this translate to your community? How will your community and your efforts create a better place to live?

Philanthropy is all about one word, GIVE! Give freely of your time, your talent and your resources. Give without asking for anything in return.

Eknath Easwaran in his book 'Like a Thousand Suns' said, "Give freely of your time, your talent, your resources; give without asking for anything in return. This is the secret of living in joy and security."

When giving comes from the heart, with sincerity, this makes the person, group or community believe that a gift has been given with no strings attached. It creates a bond within the whole community. Suddenly everyone feels a commitment to also give back and make a difference in how their community works together. Everyone helps each other and most of all, there is a sense of pride that becomes so strong that the community can begin a new way of life.

Historically, in the mid-to late 1930s, European German Jews immigrated to the United States and were considered educated, often wealthy or at least well off. This group easily built-up their entrepreneurial ideas to create worthwhile commerce in their communities. When the Russian Jews began to immigrate to the United States, the German Jews wanted to give them the opportunity to succeed even though their backgrounds were less polished. Hence, the need to create local Jewish agencies such as Family & Child Services, Jewish Community Centers and Jewish schools as outlays for giving back to the community. This concept of giving back was enhanced in other ethnic groups as well. Immigration shifted, changed and America became a bigger melting pot.

An example of a community builder is The Harry & Jeannette Weinberg Foundation that originally focused on giving back to the communities in the city and suburban areas over the years to help create a better way of life. As baby boomers began to age, it became clear to the Weinberg Foundation there was a need for unique housing facilities to handle the diverse challenges of this aging group. The Foundation has built facilities for seniors that maintain independent living as well as assisted living complexes that look after the elderly who have dementia or other debilitating illnesses. Their Foundation has also seen the need to create Senior Day Care Centers for the elderly who may not live in a care facility and instead live with their children who attend to their needs.

Philanthropy in Maryland has become a way of life for many ethnic groups. The Associated Black Charities (ABC) started by giving consideration to communities that needed an influx of assistance. They did this by bringing business men, clergy and other organizations together to raise and distribute funds to the neediest communities across the state. ABC has created dedicated strong, healthy and economically viable communities to shape better living conditions, better health facilities, and community recreational centers. They have enabled and revitalized communities to become more economically empowered.

Just before the breakout of WWII and the Holocaust, the World Jewish Relief foresaw the urgent need to save the children in the path of war. They organized Kindertransport or Kinder (Children) trains which gave parents the opportunity to help their children escape by putting them on these trains alone which were headed to Britain, Europe and beyond. I knew such a man whose life was saved by leaving his country for a new life. Let's call him Eric. He was from Austria and was put on a train at the age of 12 with other kids also traveling at the time to London. It was very scary for these children; everything was unfamiliar from the food they ate, to the language they had to learn and the fear that they would never see their parents or brothers and sisters again.

Eric stayed in London until he was 16 and then took a boat to America. He was lucky that the Jewish Family Services was there to help with living arrangements, schooling and work. Eric was able to attend Johns Hopkins University, worked and then joined the US Army. He eventually, learned several other languages and was sent oversees to Germany. He fought proudly for America and though he was kidnapped in Austria by the Germans, he was finally saved by the Americans as World War II came to an end. Unable to walk, he had to be wheel barrowed out of a concentration camp.

Upon arriving in Baltimore once again, the Associated Jewish Charities was there to help him restart his life, find work and he married. Eric became a very successful investment broker.

These two agencies alone have given families advantages they might not have had or the opportunity to participate in this type of giving back to a community. The day care centers have helped children who are taking care of their parents with varying stages of dementia giving them the opportunity to have time to take of their own needs. The strong communities created by ABC, gives parents with children educational opportunities that might not had been available without the funds for building new schools.

There are many elder facilities that have given renewed hope for many of their residents. Having a relative that is currently in an elder care facility, it is clear that the living conditions, the requirement to maintain a schedule as well as having the right medication, can almost create a new life for an aging relative. Now, there are programs created in Baltimore City that help inner city students with the opportunity to stay in places where nature abounds. These weeklong experiences give students confidence and experiences that change their lives forever. These young and impressionable children realize that there is a different world out there and it helps make them to become more productive by expanding their horizons.

These children may even start to think about careers and how they can make a better life for themselves. How they see themselves also creates a different environment for their parents. This is how local and some national philanthropists can make a difference in many communities. People interested in philanthropy, make modifications that essentially changes the direction of a community. People living in these communities see action and recognize that changes are taking place. Then, individuals in the community achieve a new personal satisfaction that may also allow some of their citizens to become philanthropists in their own right.

Many communities are often funded by philanthropists or foundations that make contributions because they may have a historical relationship with an organization or they may have an affinity to a particular mission.

A young impressionable student in Baltimore City after attending a two week outdoor nature program, may grow up to be an urban developer who realizes the importance of green space, eco-systems, play space for humans and dogs and is only interested in funding such projects. Another young person, may grow up to believe that giving back to her community means becoming a teacher and creating an after school program for children whose parents work until 6 pm.

There are those philanthropists who want to take a non-conventional approach by funding an organization that thinks out of the box, or in a start-up organization with great ideas and no money. The results are seen in cities, towns and neighborhoods with a younger population that understands, in order to move forward, they must give back to their community.

Living in a community where there is cohesiveness, character, compassion for the neighborhoods and the people that live there will make that community, town, city, state a better place to live. When a community works together to make their environment a better place to live, what begins to happen is that gangs dissolve, more productive jobs are created, young people want to stay and create an even better place to live. Everyone feels the need to help those who are less fortunate.

Many communities that have seen physical and social change take place become more effective and the economy of the community also changes. New jobs are created, more networking and peers begin to work together to make a difference for the next generation. These communities have grown to become a town and the chances that it will continue to grow are perceived as real.

If we go to back and think about the Russian Jews coming to America, they had many obstacles to overcome. Many remained in segregated communities and would not take advantage of Jewish Family Services or the English as a Second Language services that were free of charge or even ask for job assistance. There are many Russians Jews who took the step forward, started jobs, went to night school to get their GED and then became lawyers, doctors, Rabbi's, business men or real estate developers. Once they started their journey both groups had one ideal in common, they had to give back to make the next generation stronger and even better business men and women. Now, there are fewer segregated communities where Russian Jews live. They are giving more of their money to charities that resonate with their values and have become philanthropists in their own communities.

When we look back at the 'Seven Faces' of philanthropists: community activists, the devout, the investor, the socialite, the humanitarians, the benefactors and the affluent, we can see why each group has its own causes and its own tactics for giving. Each of these philanthropists all realize that there are more non-profits and foundations out there that will never be able to move forward without their assistance.

With that said, each of these 'Seven Faces' of philanthropists can still make a difference. Although, it is never really clear why some philanthropists give to some and not to other organizations, as I mentioned earlier, sometimes the mission speaks to the philanthropist or it could be they gave because they were asked. What is clear is these philanthropists really understand the need for action. However, they also realize that they have to pick and choose what they believe will be worthwhile organizations to promote.

Our goal in this book is to see what transformation philanthropy can create in one community, in one person's life or career and that every step that a person takes to give of themselves, is what really makes a difference.

Philanthropy is about the action of helping or doing for others. If you remember in Chapter 1, about finding your passion that gives you satisfaction and how you have made someone else's life stronger. What is really important is that you find what will make you get up off the couch and get out there to make a difference. Everyone in this world can be a philanthropist it just takes you to believe that when you take the time to help someone else, then they too find their passion and become a philanthropist. Remember not every philanthropist has to be rich. The richness comes from you giving back to a person or a community.

CHAPTER FOUR

WHO ARE THEY?

After coming back from a foreign country and having had the opportunity to learn another culture, I was open to learning about the athletes and how different each player really is. These baseball players come from very distinctive backgrounds, life styles, education and with different moral values. They easily learn to work as team, but at the same time when the game is over, most of them lead their own lives, often in different areas of the city. Some hangout with groupies, some go home to their families and other's just hangout alone. Overtime as the player career moves forward and they become an icon in their community, they are looked upon as real role models. The truth is, some players are and some aren't. Why is it that the fans hold the athletes to a different a standard than the average person?

What is a role model? A role model is someone who has passion and the ability to inspire others to do better; someone who has a strong set of values; a strong commitment to giving back to their community; they are selflessness and try to help others who are less fortunate and they have the ability to overcome obstacles.

These are very high standards for any human to transcend and over the last few decades, there are fewer athletes that exemplify these qualities. What do the players do that is so spectacular in order to become a role model? Hit the ball out of the park? Does that really give them privileged status? Choosing our role models should be because they have the qualities mentioned above, not because they hit the ball out of the park or make a hole in one.

There are few athletes who actually ask to be a role model and many find it more cumbersome than rewarding. Society places a very high value on athletes in general and that pressure alone can change the way a player performs on and off the field. Sometimes it seems that the standard is so high that the players force themselves to exceed their performance, which often leads to using drugs and/or steroids. Some get caught and some don't but in the end, it usually comes back to haunt them. Yet, the fans still envy the players for the 'fabulous performance' and even encourage their children to emulate these athletes. It actually seems ridiculous that when a player is caught using enhancement drugs or with an underage child or for drugs or drunken driving, it seems that the fans are astonished rather than change the role model status of that athlete.

In today's society, role models still play a huge part in sports in how young boys and girls cherish these heroes, even when their behavior may not warrant such a following. Somehow, it has become acceptable that even when athletes make off the field bad judgments they retain their role model status. The athlete doesn't realize that there is a child out there emulating the player's behavior. The athlete's bad behavior teaches the child that it is acceptable conduct to bend the rules. Bending the rules is not an acceptable action for a young child to be imitating. Athletes feel that their privileges should excuse their conduct. The reality is it only makes their behavior more deplorable. Society will only lose interest in emulating role models when the athletes realize there is no sense of entitlement for such actions.

Role models come in all shapes, sizes and personalities. Every athlete is a human being with different characteristics. Some take on the role model status as an important responsibility that encourages achievements in young children and adults. Some athletes don't take this task seriously and send a message of entitlement instead.

While, working as a sports agent, I was fortunate to see this first hand and realized that each player is a human being with good and bad personality traits. Some of their characteristics were developed during their careers. Some maximized their potential to become active in their community by giving back to the less fortunate. Others let the sense of entitlement and in some respect the sense of greed to take the forefront and they were always looking for the next opportunity to get rich quick. During my career, I was blessed to have the opportunity to work with several great athletes that really knew what it meant to be a great role model.

One of my favorite players with the Orioles was Rick Dempsey. He was a gentleman, a family man, loved to talk to school age kids and teach them about life in baseball as well as living a clean wholesome life. Dempsey was also the locker room clown and prankster. I am sure many of you remember when the tarp was put down on the field from a rain delay, seeing Dempsey emulate a homerun at home plate and then he would run the bases while doing stunts. Of course, the run from 3rd base to home always ended in a slide. His tricks on the players in the locker room are well remembered. No one was ever hurt, but things could get wild quickly and the fans loved it! Dempsey enjoyed going to schools to talk to the students about the importance of an education and learning a career that was fun and productive. Dempsey also realized that after baseball, his family and the need to make a productive living was important. He has become renowned for his ability to broadcast baseball games.

There are also players that are more behind the scenes. They choose to do good works in the community but want little to no recognition for their efforts. Doug DeCinces was just such a player. He gave back to the community in a manner that was more clandestine than public.

Doug was not your run of the mill ball player for the Orioles. First off, he was playing third base after Brooks Robinson retired from a 23-year career with the Orioles. To say the least, those were some big shoes to fill. It took a while but it turned out that Doug was a great third baseman and won the hearts of the fans. Doug knew that it was important to give back to his community and was more comfortable writing a check to an event or help pay for kids to attend a baseball camp. Doug was a behind the scenes giver and felt that it was important to have a presences in the community but he was not looking for recognition for himself. He just wanted to make a difference in whatever way he could.

Both of these players were known for their athleticism, being team players and having a clear understanding of what it means to give back. They had very distinct personalities and they gave back in the manner that made them most comfortable.

This is a very important distinction. Giving back is about what makes the individual comfortable as well as knowing what your motivating factor for giving back is. As I mentioned earlier there are several different reason why people want to give back to their communities and you should look closely at what your reason is for taking on such an effort.

How did these two players become really good role models? I am sure they learned many of these qualities at an early age. They knew what values were important in their family circle and they chose to emulate those positive qualities. Most likely, they made positive choices as they grew from teenagers, to young adults to adulthood. They also had chosen a career path that worked well for them. They were doers from an early age and realized that being a doer meant you had responsibilities that they were required to perform, whether they wanted to or not. They were never afraid to take responsibility for their actions or to admit they made a mistake. These two men were also very confident about who and what they were. With confidence comes responsibility, which begets giving back.

When you know who and what you are at an early age and know that you are most likely to participate in your community, you think ahead about the 'how' and 'why' you take on philanthropic endeavors. No one will ever ask you to become a role model, it often just happens. The players might hit back-to-back home runs, they might switch hit and get home runs each time they come to the plate or they are a great catcher or pitcher. Did they ask for this? They may have hoped this would happen and then, there they were. They did not train for it and yet they are obligated to participant in being a role model.

Sometimes life throws you a curve ball and you have a split second to make up your mind on what you are going to do. What flashes before you is your upbringing, your values and how doing the right thing feels GREAT! So, when you take on this responsibility with a vengeance you will realize you have done the right thing. What these players learned is that making a difference in a community where you are well liked, stayed ahead of the game and brought joy to a great many people, is an opportunity to really make a change.

Though you may not have any real training for this job you do see others take on this responsibility and find redemption by giving back to a community that deserves to be respected. Even when you are not in your hometown, you realize that giving back to your team's community is just as important as your responsibility to your family living on the west coast while you are playing for a team on the east coast. Your ability to bridge the gap is a blessing.

It is true that some people are born with the innate ability of giving back because it is a value that has been handed down from one generation to the next. Also, it may be that your parents saw that at early age you were special because of your superior ball playing skills. Perhaps they encouraged you to work with other players who were less fortunate or you just have a strong sense of sportsmanship. You might have been given a few breaks along the way that made you feel responsible for helping others. All these predictors are good for becoming a genuine role model in your community.

How do you start putting yourself out there, to become a pillar of your community? If you remember, getting up off the couch is the first step to making a difference in your community. Now is the time to evaluate your skills and how those skills could make a difference in helping a non-profit. You have resources that you have not yet even thought about. Start with a list of your skills and resources and make it all-inclusive.

Maybe you can't hit a baseball out of the park. I am sure your accounting skills, reading books to kindergarten children, mentoring a high school student, using your skill in Math or English as a tutor, or perhaps your carpenter skills are needed to build houses for Habitat for Humanity. Any one of these ideas could be the spark that will lift you up off the couch and start a new interest in your life. The feeling of accomplishment given to others that are less fortunate will give you the greatest gift, self-worth.

Volunteering is another avenue to become part of your community. Volunteering can often lead to a job interview either through the organization where you volunteer or because someone in that organization recommends you to another non-profit. By being a volunteer you can practice on honing your skills, it allows you to build a network and may even enhance your education with hands-on experiences.

You can also become a volunteer that works in senior day care centers, help out in a dementia unit by reading to the residents, doing art work, playing bingo or perhaps there are elderly people who are mobile but can't drive and you could drive them to their doctor appointments or help them with their groceries. Any act of kindness will give you the confidence to be a community activist.

It could be you are more inclined to just write a check to a non-profit rather than volunteering. Many people with financial capacity prefer to engage in behind the scenes giving. If this a path you choose to pursue, be sure to take your time and thoroughly analyze the organization before making a contribution. Many organizations have websites that have a rating section. It shows the rating they have received by one of the charitable resource groups that measure non-profit successes. These organizations rate the charity by how much they raise, what is their ratio of dollars-in compared to dollars-out, what is their overhead and many more components help determine if the organization is successful in fulfilling its mission.

If you are at a total loss on how to get started, think back over your childhood, through adulthood and remember the organizations that helped you. Perhaps you were a boy or girl scout, perhaps you played on a recreational team during the summer, perhaps you went to summer camp or perhaps your Dad took you to help him with his work or perhaps your Mom did volunteer work and you learned from her the need to give back.

What is really important is to start a list of ideas, do some research and make some inquiries. Even with the economy making a slight comeback, there are still many organizations that are looking for volunteers. You can become a real asset to your community.

EDDIE MURRAY

CHAPTER FIVE

BEHIND THE SCENES

Now is the time for the big guns to come out and begin talking about athletes as individuals and how and why some players believe that giving back to their community is essential to their way of life after they leave baseball.

Even though many of these athletes just want to play ball, there are those players who go out on the field every day and play their hearts out. These ball players are driven to be the best at their job.

One such player is Eddie Murray. Eddie wanted to be the best ball player. He aimed to be the best hitter and the very best first baseman for his team! He wanted to do his job every day and go back out the next day and do it all again.

Eddie grew up in the dense neighborhood of Watts in southern Los Angles, California. The community's spirit was jolted and almost destroyed in the riots of 1965. Even though Watts was considered a tough neighborhood, facing many years of hardship, the people of Watts slowly reclaimed their neighborhood after the riots.

He was the fourth eldest boy and one of 13 children, 5 boys and 7 girls. His Mom ran a very tight household, preparing the girls to be women who could run their own future household and teaching the boys how to treat women by always being respectful. All of the children used, "Yes mam," and "No sir." There was no talking to back to their parents.

Neighborhood sports were spontaneous and the five boys were always outside playing stickball in the 'sandlots' scattered throughout the neighborhood. These 'sandlots' may have been only makeshift fields that were nothing more than an empty piece of land composed of grass, dirt or sand, for Eddie they were youthful refuges for his imagination that one day he would be a major league baseball player. These sandlots were used just like in real baseball, as long as they were big enough to play the game.

Eddie progressed to playing Little League baseball under Coach Clifford Prelow, an ex-Dodger minor leaguer. Even at this young age, Eddie was known at his high school as the only senior to bat .500. Another baseball great, Osborne Earl 'Ozzie' Smith played on the same team. Ozzie went on to play in the major leagues for the San Diego Padres and St. Louis Cardinals.

All of Eddie's brothers ended up playing professional baseball at some point in their lives. Eddie always said that his oldest brother, Charles was the best hitter and Venice one of the better runners. Eddie became a great hitter especially since he could hit almost equally well from either side of the plate.

He went on to attend community college for about two years and was recruited to the minor league Orioles team in the third round of the 1973 amateur draft. He proved himself by having several very good years in the minors and Eddie made his major league debut in April 1977, playing 160 games in his first season.

I met Eddie in the summer of 1977. I remember thinking to myself he is big and tall. Being only 5'3" myself, I thought he was a giant. I also immediately noticed his caution about meeting new people. It took quite a while for Eddie to begin to trust me. Once he clearly understood my role as the 'Girl Friday' in the office and that I was there to make his life easier, we slowly and I mean slowly, began to develop a friendship.

Eddie began to develop some inroads to the community by meeting people and quickly became involved with the Headmaster, Irving Hamer, of the Park Heights Street Academy that was founded as a private high school in 1976 for kids who had been expelled or had major disciplinary issues. Eddie was impressed with Irving's ability to create a safe alternative educational environment for these children. At the time, Eddie was just starting his baseball career in the late 1970s and he was not making millions. Yet, he knew in his heart that he needed to give back to the community. Eddie grew up in similar circumstances in Watts, but was fortunate to have both parents at home and brothers and sisters that looked out for each other. Eddie quickly realized that many of the children at the Academy, lived in the neighborhood, but did not have the same home environment that he had while growing up. This realization hit Eddie hard. It was the beginning of his awareness in how lucky he was growing up and how necessary it is to help others. Irving and Eddie developed a strong connection over the years. Unfortunately, the Park Heights Academy closed and Irving returned to New York.

My working relationship with Eddie moved rather slowly. He had warmed up to me but he was still reticent when it came to trusting me. In the beginning, it was clear that the Academy was looking to use Eddie as a spokesperson however; it was quite clear to me that Eddie was not really interested in speaking in front of anyone, let alone an audience.

Remember Eddie was only 21 and had just come up to the Majors, his career and his loyalty to the job was primary in his life. When Eddie was asked to sit on the board at the Academy, he asked Irving if I could sit in for him. I was delighted to do this, though it was not in my job description as were a hundred other duties that were part of my 10-year career. It was one of my first opportunities to give back to the community.

By the spring of 1978, the Park Heights Street Academy held their big 'Thank You' lunch event. This year they hoped that Eddie would not only attend but would speak. Irving and I spoke to the Chairwoman and explained that Eddie would be delighted to attend, but he would not come up to the podium nor would he speak. I was confident that we had made it clear that Eddie and I would only attend the event. On the day of the event, Eddie and I were at the head table sitting across from each other and after a few opening remarks, Eddie was called to the podium. There was no doubt he was shocked and angry, if looks could kill, I would have been dead.

Eddie did make his way up to podium, said, "Thank You," and

immediately returned to the table. I was trying not to tear up because I was sure Eddie would never talk to me again. Irving promptly launched right in, telling Eddie that he and I had made it clear to the Chairwoman that he did not want to be called to the podium to speak. Irving reassured Eddie that this would not happen again and that he should trust that, I had nothing to do with this incident. Eddie's whole demeanor changed in an instant and I knew that Eddie and I would be trusted companions moving forward. From that, moment on Eddie entrusted me with everything. I wrote his checks, stood in for him at events when he had to be out of town for a house closing, bought jewelry for his girlfriends and the list goes on. That awkward situation turned both of our lives around and the trust between us is still there.

Eddie was also the player that gave me the name 'Hatch Lady', because I took care of everything for everybody and it was always done accurately, quickly and honestly.

Eddie was very close to his family. He worshiped his mother, respected his dad, adored his sisters and talked to his brothers constantly! He had a good heart and almost always would give his friends whatever they needed. Sometimes he was taken for granted and as time went on, he knew whom his real friends were.

He was the behind the scenes guy! He did not like the lime light, he did not like to be interviewed and he really did not like being followed by the press. During the 1983 World Series, the media turned up the heat to try to learn more about Eddie and his family. It was apparent that he only wanted to go out and play, he did not want to be interviewed and he did not want his family being molested. The press was relentless and my colleague and I decided that Eddie needed some privacy especially when the press started following him out to his home. We concluded that since he knew my parents and because they lived in a relatively secluded part of northern Baltimore County, that we would get Eddie a loaner car and he could drive out to my parent's home every night and stay there. At that very moment, Eddie became part of my family as well.

The media never really gave up on their attempts to get an interview with Eddie, but there were only a few, probably only two reporters that Eddie actually trusted. Both were writers I knew from other venues in the community and I gingerly began introducing these reporters to Eddie. There was also one photographer that he liked and trusted who also gave a great recommendation to Eddie that he could trust these two writers. Eddie really just wanted to play ball, which was always the most important thing on his mind. He never understood why his life or his family's lives were so important to anyone else. As he began slowly to trust these reporters, he did tell them that his family and his life off the field was taboo and there would be no questions answered around these two topics. Eddie understood that the fans had a huge appetite for wanting to know everything about each player and their lives; however, Eddie did not appreciate the intrusions in his life.

It was some time in the mid 1980s that Eddie's Mom passed away. Eddie was playing baseball in Japan and luckily, he was able to come back before she died. It was a hard and difficult time for Eddie and his family. I flew out to be there with him and it was the first time I had met the entire Murray clan! The boys were and still are perfect gentlemen and his sisters were wonderful. It was clear that their upbringing was guided by their Mom. After this incident, Eddie started thinking about what he could do to honor his Mom. He was already anonymously donating 33 tickets to each home ball game to inner city children. Just in case you are curious about only giving 33 tickets, #33 was Eddie's jersey number. Number 33 has not been used again since his retirement.

I had received a call from Outward Bound regarding a project they wanted to do in Leakin Park in Baltimore City as part of the Gwynn Falls Park improvements. There had been a nature center on the property for years but it needed a full makeover. I went first to check it out and then talked to Eddie letting him know that this might be the perfect opportunity to honor his Mom. We met with several board members and staff, looked at some drawings and toured around the park. At first, Eddie was too overwhelmed, but when the two of us returned for another visit, he began to soften up about the idea. A few months later, we had the groundbreaking ceremony and a year later, we had a ribbon-cutting event introducing the Carrie Murray Nature Center to the community. That park has helped thousands of children throughout the years to learn and understand nature by giving them an opportunity to really appreciate the park and its surroundings.

Eddie was adamant about being anonymous with his ability to give back to the community and even about helping his friends. His wish was to help others have an easier life, an appreciation of the world around them and have the opportunities he didn't have as a child. He would always sign autographs or stop in the street to talk a young child who was looking at him as if we were a Greek God. Sometimes he would go to schools and speak to children on the importance of an education and that being respectful to others is essential in living a clean and healthy life. He often did things his way. He loaned friends money, never asking for a promissory note of payment, he paid to have someone's car fixed and never ask for repayment. Eddie's heart was and still is big.

Over the years, he has given back selflessly with free sport camps to help young children learn the basics of baseball. Very often, he writes checks to non-profits when he feels there is a worthy cause that needs assistance. He plays in golf tournaments for non-profit organizations and is always doing things, behind the scene. He continues to be suspicious of the press but now he is rarely followed from place to place.

As we discussed in other chapters, everyone has the capacity to give back something. The important concept is to know what you really want to obtain by giving back. Do you want to be in the lime light, do you want to be anonymous, do you want to be part of what you have created or do you just give because it feels good? Not everyone has the same financial resources and not every non-profit will need the money. Volunteering can be a great equalizer for many non-profits.

Remember philanthropy comes in many forms and you might even try several ideas before you settle on one or more organizations. Being a part of something that is bigger than your everyday life creates a sense of helping your community to be a better place to live.

I have a neighbor, Nancy who worked until she was in her late sixties. Her children are grown and now she is alone. She took a few weeks off and then decided it was time to get up off the couch! Nancy started volunteering at one of the nearby hospitals, by delivering the mail, newspapers and other odds and ends that the patients needed or wanted.

Nancy also decided that she wanted to help the less fortunate and recruited another neighbor to work at a soup kitchen with her one day a week. They both enjoyed being together and their volunteerism is certainly helping others by seeing acts of kindness. Just as an aside, Nancy has been honored as the best volunteer at the hospital for the past three years!

These stories should be an inspiration for everyone to realize that often the smallest kindness can bring the biggest hope to someone less fortunate. Do you really need your name up in lights or will a simple thank you be enough recognition? The world needs to be a better place for everyone and everyone needs to stand up to become a part of making your community a healthier and happier place to live. You can make a difference in this world just by getting up, going out and finding the organizations that empowers you to do more.

RICK DEMPSEY

CHAPTER SIX

THE REAL PRANKSTER

Not every athlete or every player has the same sense humor or is consistent in the way they show up on the field to do their job and play the best baseball possible! Rick Dempsey is one of those exceptional players, playing his heart out every day, enjoying what he did and knowing that giving back to his community is a must. He was the ultimate cheerleader, which is exactly what a catcher should be doing. He had the advantage of seeing the entire field, giving the right signs to the runners, the pitching signals and indicated who should be ready for the next play. This was a great deal of responsibility and Dempsey, never walked away from any responsibility that was placed on his shoulder.

Rick was a character in his own right. He was a leader on and off the field, he lead a clean life and became a member of whatever community he was in at the time. He loved working with the young guys and keeping them in line as much as possible. Sometimes those rookies were a hard bunch to tame and he would often resort to some tactics of intimidation.

All he really wanted for the newbies was for them to understand that they were in the big leagues in real life and real baseball. Rick came to the O's in the largest trade between the New York Yankees and the O's which also brought Scott McGregor and Tippy Martinez. Rick wanted to be on a winning team and knew that the 1983 team might just be his lucky star. Sure enough, the Baltimore Orioles won the World Championship! Rick was so glad to get to the World Series that season! Who wouldn't have been!

He was the clown of the locker room and during rain delays or any time he thought it was appropriate, he would be out there doing crazy antics and making others laugh. He loved doing commercials and getting the opportunity to hang with some even funnier people. He never took life too seriously, always had an encouraging word for the rookies and great advice for the players in general. He was never considered a 'Mr. Know it All', just a catcher with a great arm and even a better eye for keeping the team on its toes.

Rick grew up in a family of four siblings and was the second oldest. His Dad was in Vaudeville and traveled around a lot. He fell in love with baseball when he was 8 while watching a World Series game and thought that was going to be him one day! Rick loved the game. He began by playing in rec leagues and was recruited right out of high school to the New York Yankees. For most of the first season, he was the backup catcher and thought he might never get the chance to play. Then he came to the O's in 1983 and that year, was his best year! Rick took his catching game really seriously and he came through with flying colors.

There is no doubt after listening to Rick's stories about his Dad that Rick's sense of humor, good looks and overall great personality were from his Dad. Rick always liked to be the good-hearted fool playing tricks and getting people to laugh. His jokes or pranks were always good-natured and never about embarrassing someone else. He liked making others laugh and putting himself in funny or compromising situations that would bring down the house!

Rick told a very funny story about his years in the junior league when his team won eight tournaments in a row. His coach had a real dynamite personality and everyone liked him. Years later when Rick was being interviewed about how he got started in baseball it came out during the interview that the coach was robbing banks in each of the eight cities the kids played in. Warner Brothers asked for the rights to Rick's story and wanted to start the movie with this anecdote. Unfortunately, as chance had it, Warner Brothers backed out!

He also felt that it was important as a recognized baseball player that he should help others to be the best they could be. Rick understood the need to give back to others and how important it had been for his career trajectory. He gave back by volunteering to visit elementary and high schools to talk about the need for a good education and on how being a 'celebrity' is not all that it is cracked up to be.

If another ball player refused to visit a hospital or help with a baseball clinic, Rick would, always 'pinch hit' and he became the go to guy on the team. If Rick got stopped in the street, he would stop, sign autographs or just chat with someone. Rick's good nature, kindness and his general overall happy go lucky attitude made him an icon in Baltimore.

It wasn't until May of 2014 that I had a chance to sit with Rick since his retirement as a player. I was lucky that I called on a day he was in town and we really had a chance to catch up with each other.

Rick is doing a multitude of things that keep him very busy. He has a pre and post TV show for the O's games and sometimes he works with Jim Palmer as a co-host announcer for the games. He also has his real estate license, making deals in downtown Baltimore. Rick has hooked up with a Jazz/R & B singer, Diana Bogart, and has recently produced two albums with her. Rick has a great voice!

His most philanthropic endeavor has been attempting to create a 501 C-3 non-profit organization called the Rick Dempsey Foundation for Shock Trauma to help raise $15 million and finish the University Maryland's Shock Trauma Unit. Rick felt strongly that the work performed by the Shock Trauma Unit was amazing and he hopes the foundation will be up and running by the fall.

Having not seen Rick in so many years, it was fun hearing about his family, exchange ideas about today's players and the trials and tribulations he had after he retired. He made his own way in the business world and seems to have succeeded. He had made no real plans career wise before he retired and at the time, it was unclear what he would do. He had started networking and connecting with people he knew in Baltimore and now on the other side of retirement he is busier than ever and making money. Rick does not get back to Los Angeles as much as he would like since he has five wonderful grandchildren, a wife and two sons still on the west coast.

What amazed me about seeing Rick now, is that he so

comfortable with who he is. Life was a series of twist and turns, ups and downs and now he has a full life with great friends and taking on new roles. We had a great conversation around his passion and commitment for the shock trauma foundation he started and how we might be able to work together.

I remember when I first met Rick, we were like kindred spirits and we got along great. I also was lucky to have a great relationship with his wife, Joani who was kind and caring. Rick became a natural for any type of promotional work or public relations opportunity that came along. He memorized scripts, made the best out of each opportunity he had and he really liked being the 'ham'. He had great jokes and could always make anyone laugh. Rick was and still is one of a kind a guy!

He never complained, never had a nasty thing to say about anyone. One of his sons played ball, which made Rick proud, but at the same time, he knew that his son was not major league material. It is difficult for a parent to squelch his son's dream. Now both of his sons are thriving businessmen.

Rick is one of the great ball players and human beings that walk this earth.

Even if you think you are shy, not funny and not very gregarious, that doesn't mean you can't give back to your community. You don't have to be a Rick Dempsey to make others feel better about their quest in life. It is most important that you take the time to find out who you are and what your passions are. Maybe it is volunteering in a vet's office because you love animals, maybe you want to volunteer at a hospital in the Neo Natal Care unit being there for premature babies that need constant contact to help them feel that someone cares, or maybe you just want to volunteer at a day care center for children under four.

Once you have found your passion or believe that you want to try something new, giving back to your community will fulfill that desire. Go out there and knock on doors, talk to your friends about your process. Speak about why you are doing this now and what it means to you. You might even be able to convince your companion that giving back to a community is an opportunity for them too. Don't get discouraged if everyone you talk to does not immediately jump at the chance. You will eventually find the right people to attract and you will have made an ever-greater impact on your community. Soon you will have the personality to attract other colleagues who will want to mimic what you have created and pay it forward as well. This is the time to step out and take a leap of faith that you are making a great deal of difference in your sphere of influence.

Not everyone is outgoing and finding the right fit might be slightly more difficult. The truth is, however, you find your passion; it will lead you to your intended path. Being comfortable within yourself is essential if you want to really make a transformation and assist others who need help to take the next step in their life. You can make a difference. You may not see the results overnight but you will see them if you look hard enough. The simplest things can change someone's life, like a smile, saying good morning, or just helping an elderly person across the street. Know that what you have done will make someone else's day better.

I have been out of the sports business for almost 30 years and yet when I saw Dempsey it was as if we had just seen each other the day before. His kindness never ceases and his love for the game has not only become stronger, he is also 100 times more knowledgeable about the game, which makes his shows so popular. I am blessed that I still have a friend in Rick Dempsey.

SCOTT MCGREGOR

CHAPTER SEVEN

THE FAMILY MAN

S ome children grow up with a really strong family foundation and other children have little or no foundation at all. Home life plays a very huge factor in a child's perception of what family life should be like.

If parents are squabbling over money, struggling to find a job or trying to scrape the money together for their child's education, this sets a tone and a precedent for how children perceive their future. Their environment also plays a role in how a child grows up. Children need structure and a strong foundation to have the confidence and the foresight to find their own way in this world. As children, we spend time at home, in school, going to church and use the immediate outdoors as our island to conquer. With this said recognition of bullying and its life long impact has become a huge issue in schools and on the playground. Peer pressure has also become a norm for many kids who feel that friends should have more influence over them than their own parents should.

Scott McGregor had a very stable and strong foundation growing up. His parents knew the importance of creating a strong family base in which to raise their children. The father-son relationship was essential and a forgone conclusion in how the McGregor children were raised. Scott knew he was loved and knew what was important to his parents. This loving environment created the man he was to become. Scott loved baseball and having his Dad as a coach for the Giants only increased his enthusiasm for the sport. His foundation, his values, his mission to be a good Christian and a good father himself, propelled him to be a better son and father later in life.

Scott had a great deal to give to his community and knew that he was not interested in creating new community efforts when there was so much philanthropy already taking place in his town. He believed that giving children a real shot of love, honesty, joy and by instilling a consciousness about who they are and what they want to be, would help them become better individuals in their communities. He taught that a community is about living a life where you not only provide for your own family but also provide what is needed in the overall community. This outlook creates togetherness and caring for their community that might not have otherwise been taught.

Children follow by example and lead only when they become self-confident in leadership. There was no need for Scott to create his own non-profit foundation or even to start new programs to promote father-son events. He was more interested in enhancing the programs that already existed in his community that encouraged youth to live by the same example he portrayed while giving back to his community.

Scott was a strong believer in having children and young adults learn through example. Often in a community, there are already charitable opportunities which need volunteers for after school programs, sports events, tutoring and mentoring. These charities need help with creating an atmosphere of opportunity to strengthen and keep a community vibrant. There is really no need to re-create what is already in place. What is needed is for you to get up off the couch and learn about the opportunities in your own community that will make a difference.

Charity is often expressed as compassion for the underdog, pure kindness towards your fellow man and understanding and sympathy for others. It comes in many forms, from taking an elderly person to their doctor's appointments, to coaching a little league team, to creating events for children with special needs.

As early as six years old, Scott loved baseball. He started playing just as soon as he could hold a bat. It helped that his Dad was a baseball coach and his community environment back in the 1950s lent itself to more time outdoors. Baseball seemed like 'the sport' to be playing. Children didn't watch TV all hours of day and they didn't have computers so being outside in the fresh air was the thing to do. By the time, Scott was six he was playing against nine year olds and it became clear that he had an exceptional throwing arm. He was always a pitcher and loved the game even more than going to school. He was a quick study and soon learned that the scouts were following him. While growing up and playing high school baseball together, one of his baseball buddies was George Brett another baseball legend, who had a distinguished 21-year baseball career playing with the Kansas City Royals as third baseman.

Even though Scott was a good student, he knew that being a major league pitcher was going to be his goal in life. He had no desire to go to college and was drafted right out of high school by the Yankees. His dream of winning a World Series was at the top of his wish list. He played in the minors for three years. When he was called up to the big leagues and traded along with Tippy Martinez, Rudy May, Rick Dempsey and Dave Pagan to the Orioles, he thought his chances of winning a World Series ring were gone. Little did he know, he would go on to win a 1983 World Series ring.

McGregor fit right in with the Orioles. He had a great pitching arm, made friends easily and fell right in line with the pranksters of the locker room. Because of Scott's strong family foundation, he had a formidable character and a strong work ethic. These strengths were a good fit with the Orioles way of doing business. He was married, eventually had three children and created a family life very similar to how he grew up. He could not have imagined a better life for him and his family.

The Orioles were quite community oriented and often called on the players to visit the Children's Hospital, Shock Trauma Unit, schools, banquets and church groups. Some of the players joyfully did these events, yet it seems that Scott went more than most. Scott knew the importance of family and that it is was essential to give back to a community when you are made a hero and a person to look up to. He was a clean cut, down to earth man who wanted to be known for his abilities and to have a strong presence in his community. He enjoyed going to events where he could make others feel better about their lot in life and if he could make a child smile, or an adult sit up and take notice, he felt he had used his time wisely.

As a player, Scott took his job as an Oriole, a father, a husband and a pillar of the community very seriously. He was also raised to be a good Christian and started a Bible study with one of his teammates, Pat Kelly. Neither of them felt compelled to push their religion on anyone who was not interested. Scott and his wife found a church near their home and both became long time congregants. They felt that raising a family with a strong religious background was an important foundation for their children. Their religious values and giving back to others were important lessons for his children.

Being that Scott had a strong family foundation with loving and attentive parents he knew the value of giving back to the community. As a child, he and his Dad attended many father-son events and Scott felt that those events gave him a great perspective on how to create a strong father-son relationship for his own family. Scott would often take his boys to these types of events when he was called upon to attend and speak. Though his sons were not baseball players, Scott and his wife felt that being outside was a great way for their kids to learn about the kind of neighborhood they were living in and how important it was to have strong values that created a clear vision on where they wanted to go in their lifetime.

He felt that his life had allowed him to raise a wonderful family, play great baseball, win a World Series ring and find a church that gave the best life possible to his children as they matured. He was a loving and caring father and understood that the world his children grew up in was not as idyllic as the one he and his wife knew. Scott and Cara believed that their religion would carry them through any crisis they might have to face as a family. The Church gave them solace and allowed the family to move through difficult periods. Scott had the foresight and knowledge that by giving back to the church and to the community this would help him and his family have a better place to live.

The McGregor's did not have large sums of money nor were they in debt. In their family, the children came first and the community next. Indeed their influence in the community was felt by many people. They offered comfort and assisted people in need, especially if there were children. Scott gave his time to athletic leagues, baseball summer camps and continued attending father-son events when asked. He enjoyed visiting sick children and spoke anywhere where he could, on motivating children to do better in everything they wanted do. When speaking, all he needed to do was to tell the story the way it was. Stories are great for kids to hear because they almost always pull at your heartstrings and send a strong message to children that life can be better as you grow up.

Scott did not want to start a foundation. Instead, he desired to make people see the real life changes when a homeless person felt good about him/herself or about a young boy who wanted to play baseball and had no equipment by finding an angel that was willing to help.

There are plenty of these stories that motivate someone to get up off their couch and make a difference. There are countless venues where you can find pathways to pursue that will give you the satisfaction of knowing you are helping someone in need. There are so many agencies that need help. Do some research on what might interest you and make an appointment to visit the organization that could help you learn the local customs. Trying to find the right fit for you, may take a while. Keep in mind the end goal is the impact that you will make on a child or an adult.

Remember, giving back is a part of your life. It is a way to feel alive, vibrant and creative while helping someone in need. There are so many organizations to choose from that it is sometimes overwhelming. You may choose to shut down and go back to your couch however, this is not acceptable behavior. Your need to give back should be stronger than the need to stay in one place. Giving back is important for the equilibrium of your community. It ensures that a community grows and expands for the betterment of everyone.

If you have only one choice to make about who to help, think about working with children. Kids are very impressionable especially up to the age of five. Reading out loud to them, taking them on field trips, showing them how to get to the library and what it is, can make a huge difference in someone's life. Working with children is not only investing in their future it makes their community a better place. With children, you are helping to build a strong foundation and hopefully these children will grow up and continue with building a strong foundation for the next generation.

JIMMY JONES

CHAPTER EIGHT

THE CONNECTOR

Networking and mentoring is a wonderful opportunity in really getting to know people in your community. What that does it mean to have a community?

Community is referred to as a social group that has shared and common values, or has the same interests or passions.

Belonging to a community is an opportunity to share ideas, thoughts, a personal vision you would like to pursue or the shared vision for a group. By participating in a community, you can build a team or a network of people who can connect you with other people in different communities, which in turn gives you the opportunity to do more networking.

Networking is about bringing different people together to exchange information, get answers to questions, share ideas and passions and often, find help in knowledge or expertise that you do not have. Networking creates an occasion that allows you to expand the boundaries or limitations of your community.

I was working at Johns Hopkins University as the Director of Development for the Krieger School of Arts and Sciences and after working there for about a year a friend of mine, suggested that I meet Jimmy Jones who was the new Vice President of Human Resources. When I met Jimmy, I had no idea that he was a retired football player until we had lunch one day and we each briefly spoke about our backgrounds. Right there in that moment we created our own community, expanded on who we knew and how we could help each other. This is really what networking is all about, expanding your community to help others with their job or help them to move forward on their career path. By getting to know a new friend who has been introduced into your community, you have the opportunity to broaden your horizons and learn that there are people out there who can help you.

Connecting with Jimmy was very interesting. Even though we had similar interests, he knew very little about the actual practices used in fundraising and I knew very little about human resources. This gave us the opportunity to learn more about each other. As we got to know each other, it was clear that both of us were organized, detail oriented and decision makers.

After, Jimmy asked me to sit on a committee to recruit a candidate for human resources in the School of Arts and Sciences I began to have a better understanding of the qualifications needed to be in human resources. He also invited me to participate on the grievance committee. The committee gave employees the opportunity to register their displeasure over a staff incident that they felt was out of line with the way staff should be treated.

Though Jimmy had done some philanthropic work in his hometown, he had not really done any fundraising. We often spent time discussing the process needed to cultivate a prospect and how to eventually make 'the ask'.

We also discussed his career path as a professional football player. Jimmy had a rather eclectic educational and athletic career. He started playing tackle football at 6 years old at the YMCA and continued playing throughout high school. Then he went to college at the University of Nebraska. As an athlete Jimmy played football, baseball, ran track and field, wrestled and could slam-dunk a basketball!

When Jimmy was drafted in 1966, by both leagues, (NFL & AFL) he signed on with and played for the New York Jets, but at the end of the season, he had a knee operation, which was the first of four operations. Jimmy's professional football career ended in 1974. He has remained an avid fan, attends reunions and has always helped retired or and up and coming players with their careers. Because of his distinguished football career, Jimmy was also a four-time Hall of Famer.

He grew up in Morristown, New Jersey and started a paper route when he was 8 years old. Since he participated in football, basketball, wrestling and track and field, there were some days that he would wrestle right after school and then go off to play basketball in the evening or vice versa.

His Dad drove an oil truck and his Mom cleaned houses and did laundry. The family had an advantage in that they owned their home, which was uncommon in those days. The story behind owning their own home was that his great grandfather worked for James Buchanan Duke who started Duke University, Duke Power and Light and several other companies. When he died, he left his money to his daughter and Jimmy's great grandfather, who was originally from South Carolina and was raising 15 children. With that inheritance, his great grandfather was able to give each one of his 15 children enough money to buy their own home. That house was passed down to Jimmy's grandfather and then to his father. In many ways, it was a blessing for the entire family!

During the off season, Jimmy was very involved with the United Way. He was going to hospitals to visit the children, he became involved with the Big Brothers and Big Sisters program and when he returned home, he became very involved with the Seeing Eye project that trained dogs to help the visually impaired. The Seeing Eye program was in fact the first program of its kind in the country and started in Morristown, New Jersey in the late 1920s. While working with the United Way it also gave Jimmy the opportunity to learn about payroll deductions and how he could designate his deductions to the charity he wanted to support.

Eventually, Jimmy and his wife, Janet started a scholarship program, The Janet Watkins Jones Scholarship for students who were good athletes but not a Division 1 level player. In order to maintain athletic budgets and Division 1 status, competition is fierce amongst these schools offering a limited number of full or partial scholarships and only to the best young athletes. Together, Jimmy and Janet started their non-profit with $25,000 and over the next 25 years; they gave scholarships to over 40 graduating seniors each year. The Janet Watkins Jones Scholarship continues helping young athletes attain their goal.

Because of his community commitment, Jimmy was well known and he was great at engaging corporations and local businesses to support the scholarship program. He was an excellent networker and was always engaging others to become involved with his fundraising ventures.

Over the years, Jimmy's priorities shifted and his focus turned to helping others in need in Africa. Jimmy connected with President Clinton who was very concerned about the high percentage of AIDS in Africa. After meeting with President Clinton, Jimmy and his wife left for Lesotho to fight AIDS. He was fortunate once again with his networking skills and worked with Reebok to send tennis shoes, rackets and outfits to Jimmy while he was in Lesotho.

He started a program to teach children more about AIDS and the dangers that exist in their country. As an incentive to take the classes, anyone who completed the program was able to choose a gift sent by Reebok. They were also instrumental in developing a Strategic Plan for the government that ensured doctors, nurses and educators would learn their new roles in fighting AIDS. Jimmy helped to save lives.

Jimmy believes that giving back was a forum for him to learn about becoming an adult that started with his parents' values. Even with very modest financial means, his parents always seemed to have enough food at every meal for any child who needed to eat. The Jones' house was a gathering place for children to come, play and get a meal. Jimmy understood at an early age that giving back and connecting with people to build a network of guidance was important. It became the means that allowed him to evolve, to grow, give back and create a community that he could be proud of and continue to nurture.

Having made a connection with Jimmy almost 25 years ago, our alliance remains strong. We have the ability to continue to help each other with networking and charitable giving. Jimmy had also become involved with a non-profit outside of Morristown, called The Sharing Village.

This group was assisting disabled children to learn how to drive a horse buggy in harness racing. It gave these children experience in 'being normal' and while learning to care for their horses these children had a sense of accomplishment. Jimmy began with helping with personnel issues, some branding and marketing and realized that they needed someone to assist them with fundraising. He did not hesitate to pick up the phone and ask me if I would meet with the group. He knew I'd say yes, just as I know that if I needed a similar favor from him, he'd be there for me. Networking is a two way street and certainly gives multiple satisfaction to both the giver and the taker!

Over the years, Jimmy has remained involved in his hometown community and continues to give back even to this day. He does it in just about any capacity he has to offer. A few years ago, Jimmy and his family started his own local taxi business and he probably gives out more free rides than he has paying customers using the taxi service. His goal was to provide a service for the elderly, the infirm and for youngsters with parents who often can't provide transportation to school or a sporting event.

Jimmy has always been generous with his time, speaking with up and coming athletes about the challenges they will face as they move up the ladder. He has made a difference in his community and he feels that his scholarship program was the best program he and his wife could have created because it gives students an opportunity to play sports in college. It most likely changed the lives for many of those students and let's hope that they are giving back to their communities in return because of what Jimmy did for them.

The experiences in Lesotho gave him a new perspective on how to engage people in another country and the difference they were able to make for the entire country. They gave the government a five-year strategic plan that would set in motion a program for HIV/AIDS testing for everyone in the country.

Janet and Jimmy also sponsored two young women from Burkina Faso to reside in their home and go to college. The young girls who are now women, completed graduate school and are gainfully employed.

Jimmy was not a wealthy man, fundamentally he understood and cared about giving back, to make someone else's life easier. Anyone who has the will and the need to give back can do this. You don't have to have wealth. What you do need is compassion for others and the desire to assist another person with a better life for their family and their community. If you are passionate about seeing your community grow and become a beacon of light for its residents, you will delight in being an agent of change.

You may have taken the time and energy to help someone in need who may very well become the next millionaire in your community. Remember, this is not about the money. It is about the personal satisfaction you have knowing that you made a difference in someone's life. You got up off that couch, took stock of your abilities and made this a better day for someone else.

PAM SHRIVER

CHAPTER NINE

A YOUNG START

Growing up in the 60s was an era of discord, with changes in societal ideas that added more confusion for the youth of this generation. There were so many different and new ideas floating around from flower power to protests against the Vietnam War that no one really knew what to do.

Teenagers were growing up faster, were more belligerent, uncooperative towards their parents and they were no longer satisfied with movies that represented the 'good old days'. Certainly many felt that school and college was not for them. For some parents their ideas shifted to either being more liberal or more conservative in their views. Children of all ages felt they had the right to do what grown-ups did. Teens were ready to smoke marijuana and cigarettes or start drinking alcohol while parents were unclear as to how much they should reign in their children or if they should be more permissive. Peer pressure got worse as did the drugs and drinking. It seemed that no one was taking charge. It was not an easy transition to swing the pendulum back to center and start some new trends once again.

Still there were those parents who were able to talk to their children as if they were adults and at the same time attempted to impart the values and the foundation that their parents had been taught when they were children. These parents knew that in each generation there had been the 'Nay Sayers', the hippies, the drug addicts, the ones who didn't want to finish school or college and certainly did not want to work for a living. Society has a way of leveling itself out and has the 'goody two shoes' to re-engage with the right values.

Pam Shriver just so happened to be one of those. She was settled, had strong values and was raised with an even stronger family foundation. It did not even occur to her to rebel or run off and do something wild or weird. Her family life was filled with kindness towards each other, caring and giving and a strong respect for her parents. Most weekends included a family outing that even included her grandparents. Every family member played tennis, swam and sat together for meals with civilized discussions. Pam enjoyed the togetherness, the camaraderie of being part of a family that relished each other and she appreciated the care, understanding and advice that came from her parents. Pam knew that her parents were engaged in the community whether volunteering at a hospital, assisting in school activities or donating to a local charity.

It was a time of experimentation for teens and they took full advantage trying everything that their parents thought was inappropriate for them. It was a time to take action and get these children back on track. Parents fought to instill values that would serve their children for the rest of their lives. Being a 'rebel without a cause' was a concept that the 60s generation believed should be adhered to in order to be accepted by their peers.

On the other side, parents wanted their children to learn to be better citizens in the community and take actions that would give them the stability and ingenuity to give back as adults. The more those parents could teach by example with the same values and insights they had growing up, then the better this generation would become in building a strong and healthy community.

Pam knew at an early age that she loved playing tennis not just, because it was a family event, but because she had great eye-hand coordination and the more she practiced the better, she played.

She attended the prestigious McDonogh School that originally started out as a semi-military run school for boys in 1873 and later became co-ed in 1975. She thoroughly enjoyed her time there especially because her tennis improved exponentially when she started playing against the boys at school. As her eye-hand coordination improved, she became more confident and began to realize that she had what it took to one day be a professional tennis player. This thought was overwhelming and exhilarating at the same time. Another very interesting occurrence was that her parents knew and understood her love for the game and never pushed or persuaded her to become a professional. Being a tennis professional wasn't discussed until her coach came to talk to her parents about Pam's natural ability in the game and her incredible potential. She had won a variety of tournaments in and around Maryland and was gaining quite a reputation. Her parents upon hearing this news, only encouraged Pam to do what she felt was the right thing for herself. Pam appreciated the confidence and the openness her parents gave her to make her own decisions.

Pam was a go-getter at school and made lots of contacts, that would one day become a part of her sphere of influence throughout her life. These contacts were significant over the years, because Pam understood that no one moves ahead without connections. Her ability to cover the court with her reach, determine where the ball would be in advance of the free fall and her quick reflexes, gave her an opportunity to transcend her game to the next level. She also wanted to remain a part of the Baltimore community and could do so by playing great tennis. Having made connections over the years with many of her classmates and other members of the community, in 1986, she was able to create the Pam Shriver Tennis Challenge in Baltimore, which continued long after her retirement from tennis.

In 1978, at the early age of 15 ½, she declared that she would play her first professional tournament as an amateur and at 16 defeated Martina Navratilova the then Wimbledon champion, in a semifinal at the women's singles. Pam proved to everyone on the circuit that she was a force to be reckoned with and only lost to the seasoned professional, Chris Evert in the final. In only six months after her run to the finals of the US Open as a teen, she turned professional and graduated one year early by condensing her junior and senior years of high school.

It is notable that Steffi Graf who started her full professional career in 1983 and Monica Seles who began her pro career in 1989 superseded Pam. All four were the youngest girls to enter the circuit competing throughout most of Pam's career and all became great players. Pam saw the value of camaraderie among these young women, even though they were rivals on court because each one was all about the love of the game. Pam held true to the values her parents instilled in her and believed that she would be a better player and friend to others by adhering to the those values. She believed that she would be a world-renowned professional tennis player and by 1983, she was holding a singles ranking of #3 in the world.

Pam knew at a relatively early age that giving back was a part of her family's values. She watched her mother go to elder care facilities to help deliver food, read to the patients or just be there to help out at a moment's notice. This was Pam's first introduction to the concept of giving back to her community. It was one she never forgot.

She had solid ideas about how she wanted to live her life and how her own family would be once she left the tennis world. She knew that she would find ways to give to her community. As mentioned earlier she started the Pam Shriver Tennis Challenge that was an annual event for 25 years in Baltimore and the monies raised were given to charity.

Pam continued to make great contacts and increased her networking circle. She became great friends with many of the women and men on the circuit and remained in touch with them over the years. She was grateful for her good fortune that many of them agreed to play in her charity events she held in Baltimore. Pam's energy, kindness and understanding of the importance of giving back to her community, allowed her to engage tennis professionals that often would not have been interested in playing in such an event. Her love for the game was such a motivation for her, as well as the good she was doing for her community.

Pam then moved to Los Angeles and she began to assist with charity events in southern California. She also became a well-known tennis analyst and broadcaster giving her a continuous outlet for her talent to do something besides just play tennis. Pam really enjoyed meeting new people, giving them pointers or learning about their individual skill set. This made her traveling much more fun.

Her education and time spent learning her skills at McDonogh have lasted and been put to good use throughout her tennis career and beyond. She went to a school that was progressive, and small enough to have given her the opportunities to learn about her abilities as an athlete at a rather early age. The school also sustained her with friendships that she still cherishes today while sitting on the Board of Trustees and other committees. Pam believes that this form of giving back is not only about the education but it is also about giving back to the community that originally gave to her. It is being able to return the gesture as it was given to her and knowing that this can be seen as an example that is passed on from generation to generation. This concept of giving back has also been the fuel for volunteering at her children's school in LA. Pam feels that it is important that she be a part of their education, learn the school's inner workings and find out what the school's needs are in order to help.

Pam is very generous and though she has a huge volunteer footprint in Baltimore and LA, she feels the urge to do more. In both cities, she has utilized a particular philanthropic vehicle called a donor-advised fund. These funds are held with a bank or non-profit entity that in turn facilitates Pam's charitable giving in her communities and or to causes of her choice. Donor–advised fund contributions are not only convenient and safe they can be sent to any non-profit globally. Pam continues emulating the lessons in charitable giving that her parents taught her.

Pam is also a board member of a non-profit that Matt Stover, the retired Baltimore Ravens kicker started, called The Players' Philanthropy Fund (PPF). It is a donor-advised fund platform that assists professional athletes with safe and secure charitable giving to causes in the communities of the donor's choice. She is a volunteer for PPF but she also has her donor-advised fund there as well.

If you have taken, the time to get up off your couch and begin to take in the lessons Pam shares about connections, networking and the gathering together of friends and family, you too could make a difference in your community. It is not that difficult to step out of your comfort zone with people you have been associated with for 20 plus years. Take the step to see if you and any of your contacts need assistance or want to collaborate with you on a worthwhile project that you both like. So many non-profits out there need volunteers or a charitable gift. Working alongside a colleague, will perhaps give you the opportunity to rekindle an old friendship as well as have the opportunity to make a difference in several people's lives. The personal rewards, so outweigh the scariness. Everyone needs a friend to take those first steps to reach your own comfort level as a philanthropist.

There is so much you can do to reward yourself and others when these first steps are taken. Think about all the places that might not have needed help when you were a teenager but need assistance today. Most likely, there will be at least one person who is still there, remembers you and can give you an update on not only their organization, but also other non-profits that might need volunteers or that charitable gift. Be creative, call all your classmates that still live in town and ask them to attend a networking event to lend a hand to others in need. Make a list of the activities or the organizations you knew about while growing up in your hometown and pay them a visit today. Meet the Executive Director, talk to the staff, find out what they need most and begin to recruit from your connections, friends, family and even from the organization that may help this non-profit. This will give you, your group of volunteers and others the opportunity to make a real difference. Getting up off that couch will feel GREAT!

ANDREA SEEFELDT KNIGHT

CHAPTER TEN

BREAKING BARRIERS

Passion is something that everyone wants and everyone needs it to get their own thought processes flowing. Passion can really get you up off that couch to spread the word about what you want to accomplish. Where does that passion come from?

It can start with a seed that is planted by going to the library and reading about non-profits and the different organizations that really care about helping others less fortunate. That seed can get you excited about being a mentor or as a sponsor for Big Brothers or Big Sisters. The manifestations of your passion are the results you see over time in the life of a child, an adult or an organization. When you see a child grow, learn, feel self-confident and then looks up to you with gratitude and thanks, your life will be changed as well. Confidence is the most important feeling we can give someone less fortunate. Passion becomes our driving force; it gives us happiness and self-worth. It is not work; it is a blessing!

Andrea Seefeldt Knight told me she was born loving horses even though she did not see a horse before she was about four. She just knew her passion was horses and always would be. She thought the look and the feel of a horse was majestic. Watching a racehorse circle a track is even more marvelous as the horses' bunch together, whips are flying, and jockeying for position on the track and every jockey's passion is the WIN! Each horse has its own personality and some racehorses have a real 'heart' for running the race. Racing runs in the horse's blood and they know – they really know that what they have to do is win. Not winning is not for lack of trying, another horse can just be faster. This appreciation of horses and how they run to win was what gave Andrea the impetus to chase her own dream of being a jockey. It was not an easy life wanting to be a woman jockey. She faced ridicule from the male jockeys, no agent wanted to help her and even the owners and the trainers were not her advocates. Her passion for horses is what kept her going and because of that, she was able to reach her goal.

Andrea and her brother were latch key kids even before those terms existed in our vocabulary. They were responsible for cooking and cleaning the house. Their parents were both professors at the University of Maryland and they worked long hours to be able to give their children their dreams. Andrea and her brother became involved with the 4-H club near where they lived and eventually were given ponies by their parents. Through 4-H they began competing in a few events for hunters and jumpers.

Andrea's brother then took a job at Bowie Racetrack where he became a groomer and she followed him to the track taking an entry-level job of Hot Walker. Since all, racehorses need to train every day, but not always in a race, the Hot Walker would walk alongside the horse for exercise or until it was cooled down after a work out and the coat was dry. Depending on how many sprints and how lathered the horse is determines how long the horse is walked. Typically, the horse is walked for 25-35 minutes and then given a sponge bath. Most of time the trainer or someone else who worked on the horse regularly, informed the Hot Walker what the next steps were for that horse. There, a 'jockey want-a-be' known as Exercise Riders or full-fledged Jockeys were given instruction from the owner or trainer on how to ride the horses.

Thoroughbreds race about once every 3 weeks and in between races, they need to train daily to stay fit. To remain in competitive condition the horse is either jogged, galloped or breezed. A breeze is when the horses are asked to go almost full out racing to gain or maintain their optimum fitness. Every breeze is clocked to see when a horse tires and the length of time it lasts as a forerunner.

Andrea's mother was most likely one of the first feminists on the University of Maryland campus. Andrea credits her mother's go and do attitude, assertiveness and overall willingness to be exactly who she was, as a great role model for her. Andrea had to work harder and longer than any male jockey ever needed just to get started. Her confidence and passion for horses were her driving factors and these kept her in the racetrack arena for over 20 years. She knew what she wanted and she went after it with a vengeance that forced her to take care of herself and never give up. Situations may have been difficult but she overcame every obstacle.

Never giving up and following her passion, kept Andrea on track. She also had taken a job at Bowie but was only allowed to walk the horse after it had just breezed. Andrea was a Hot Walker for a year, exercised horses for another year and then was a jockey for 13 years after she had been riding for 8 years. She remembers her first ride as exhilarating!

Andrea loved to ride and was fearless even with all her injuries. First of all, she only stands about 5'7'' and her riding weight was 105 pounds. Getting up on a horse that is 15 to 17, hands high felt like being a midget on the back of a giant. Then to take off at lightning speed around an oblong racetrack with dirt and dust flying, it is a miracle she could even stay on the horse.

As Andrea became more proficient at being a jockey, there were other obstacles to overcome. Just as in any industry for singing, dancing and acting, one has an agent, but few agents were willing to work with Andrea. The trainers and owners didn't necessarily shut her out; they just gave her the worse horses to ride, the ones the boys didn't want. At some point, Andrea realized she had to be her own agent. She was fearless while speaking to as many trainers and owners as she could to get them to understand and even observe her talents as a jockey.

As she rode at the various tracks, it became clear to one trainer, Richard W. 'Dickie' Small that she was talented, bright, knew how to handle all types of horses and she loved being a jockey. In 1989, Dickie took her on as one of the first female jockeys riding for a very established trainer. Andrea did not let him down. Her attention to details on the various tracks she raced on, gave her an advantage. She was astute to how the tracks were running because she knew most of the jockeys and how they raced and which horses were better on a fast or slow track. The trainer and the owner always gave the jockey's their instructions, but many jockey's did what they thought was going to get them to the finish line first. Andrea and Dickie always collaborated about which horse would be best to ride in the race, how to ride the race and their partnership often ended in wins. Andrea poured her heart into racing, winning 120 races for Dickie and becoming the first female to win the Pennsylvania Derby.

She was only the third woman to compete in the Kentucky Derby and the second female in the Preakness. In all, she rode in 6,251 races and won 604. She had a very good career with a very rough start. As any jockey knows, they are prone to injuries and Andrea was no exception. Her injuries entailed a broken pelvis, ribs, a collarbone, crushed vertebrae (now she only stands at 5'6" and weighs about 125), a torn kidney, broken toes, teeth through the lip and many other ailments. She retired in 1994 because her body was just worn out. As a retirement present in 1994, Dickie gave Andrea a painting of her final winning race.

Andrea had her come back in the first Lady Legend Race at Pimlico in Baltimore, Maryland in 2010. She wanted to get back in the game and with some trepidation, she did, while surrounded by all of the retired women jockeys who also returned to ride in the race. Andrea never lost her love for horses and this passion kept her full of love and caring for horses. She came back with intent and purpose because this had been her passion for most of her life. She did not harbor any resentment or ill will towards anyone. Andrea had always wanted to be a jockey and feel the thrill of the ride. It is so rewarding do be able to do the one thing in life that you love the most. There had been plenty of disappointments, many injuries and many trials and tribulations over the years, but she never once wanted to throw in the towel.

Andrea took the Lady Legend Race very seriously. In advance of the race, for three months she rode every day at sun up and got back to her jockey weigh of 112. This was not only important to her it was the first time retired women jockeys were being showcased. She was somewhat mortified about riding after being in retirement. Andrea was delighted to see that all the money from that race and the next four consecutive races went to the Susan G. Komen for the Cure a foundation that focuses on public health education, screening and research to fight breast cancer.

Her ideas on giving back to the community were visiting hospitals, supporting the Shock Trauma Unit, going to schools to talk to children and from time to time, she stepped out of her comfort zone to do a fashion show when knowing that the money was to support a community organization. She knew the importance of giving back and felt that though she had won many races; those earnings did not go very far to help others. She had also used one of the horses she got through Dickie Small to help teach riding from time to time. She looked forward to riding for money in the Lady Legend because the funds would go to help cancer patients and make a difference for many women. The fashion shows were a real stretch for Andrea because the tomboy in her was so strong, but once she understood that the money was going towards making women's lives better, she felt it was worth her stepping outside of her comfort zone.

Because we are talking about getting interested in volunteering and the obstacles, you might want to find your own mentor to assist you in this endeavor. Andrea found Dickie Small who was willing to give her a chance and she did not let him down. If you think about the people you have known over the years, there is most likely someone who is willing to help you get over the obstacles. Don't be afraid to ask. What is the worst that can happen?

The person says, "No thank you, however; here is the name of a friend that I will ask if he/she would be willing to help." Instead of thinking that this is begging, it is really seeking advice and assistance. Many people will say, "Yes," because they remember when they were young once and that they too were helped.

It was very interesting to me when I was interviewing Andrea, that we had so many things in common. Both of us are somewhat small in stature, we love horses and we have a huge 'can do' attitude. We were never afraid to stick out our necks. We believed we could do anything and never gave it a second thought. What was different was the person that influenced our lives at an early age. Andrea's mother was her role model and my Dad was mine. Yet, they both projected onto us the concepts that it is better to be a leader instead of a follower, that you must be trustworthy and honest and always keep forging ahead. In addition, Andrea's mother was very forthcoming with advice on the actual deliverance of a strong woman role model. My Dad gave me more advice through osmosis and I was just supposed to understand the information being sent to me. Regardless, Andrea and I had an interesting upbringing.

Anyone reading this book by now will understand that the information is directed at you. Now there should be an understanding that making a difference in someone's life makes you a better person. These stories give you a starting point to branch out and make your community a better place to live. You can start making an impact on your friends and family. Explaining to others how to become involved in helping others, will give them a chance to change their lives and a community's image. You should take the time to really shine and do something that will give you, another person or an organization a fresh start.

Once you take the time to find an organization or decide to be a mentor to someone else, you will respect yourself more and respect the people and organizations around you. Having done some research through the library about various organizations, you will have an appreciation about why non-profits are important and why volunteering, mentoring, being a Big Brother or Big Sister makes such a difference. Everyone needs to feel wanted, important and cared for whether you are an individual or running a business. Your attitude about assisting others will make you and your community a better place to live.

CHAPTER ELEVEN

LEARNING A TRADE

Every family unit has different values and morals that are imparted to the next generation and there are some invariable aspects that do not change. Music is one of these aspects that have not changed, when parents say, "Our music was not that loud and not that graphic."

The truth is that every generation has its own values to create and live by. It is interesting to note that some families make it really clear how their children are raised and instill in their children the values they had growing up. However, there are parents who only imply to their children how they should act and behave. This is mostly done through osmosis, observation of the parents' behavior which goes hand-in-hand with, "Do what I say, not what I do." This leaves kids in a quandary as to how they should be acting. Children need structure that teaches them to learn by example instead of making it up as they go along. When this happens, it implies that the child may have to make their own set of values and morals.

It is unlikely that many families raise their children with the same underlining principles as the house next door. Opposing values, principles and actions promote an atmosphere of confusion for children as their sphere of influence begins to change while growing and developing. Parents who promote unconditional love, involvement in sports, volunteer activities, teaching the meaning behind holidays like Thanksgiving, Father's and Mother's day, Christmas, Hanukah and Kwanza, are setting the ground work for their children. These children will later understand the need for sharing their attributes and knowledge with others who may be less fortunate.

Parents who speak to their child with open-ended questions will allow the child to begin figuring out the difference between moral dilemmas. These moral impasses may end up creating a split with some of their peers. Children rebel mostly as teenagers because peer pressure can be more enticing and exciting than what is taught by their parents. This becomes a time when rebellion may be more than the family can handle resulting in a huge split within the family unit.

As teenagers move into adulthood, their values and morals often change or are forgotten because they move in very different circles as a teenager as compared to college. This creates a schism in their values, morphing into something unfamiliar from the manner in which they were raised. Some people need a nudge from a colleague, clergy, instructor or an older adult to get them to revert back to what their values and morals were as a child or to adopt empathetic and caring principles. Giving back to your community is not as easy as waking up one morning saying, "I am going to give back to my community today!"

Many of the athletes in this book had role models that nudged them into seeing the benefits not only for themselves but for the people they could help. This is not always an easy realization for someone who has lost their job and thinks they will never find another job.

As I have stated in this book several times, if you just make an effort to remember what you may have done as a child. Remembering how you helped others with good sportsmanship, helped out a friend with his/her homework, showed a friend how to throw a football, dribble a basketball or hit a ball with a bat, which are acts of giving back and these acts gave you a sense of satisfaction.

If you remember the Eddie Murray story and when he met the Executive Director of the Park Heights Street Academy, it was Eddie's first introduction to philanthropy. The Executive Director gave Eddie the nudge he needed to see that giving back to these students would make huge a difference in their lives.

Eddie grew up in Watts and he played sandlot ball for years. Someone saw Eddie's potential and gave him the opportunity to play baseball. Eddie in turn saw that these children in Baltimore's inner city needed a boost with their own path. Eddie was there to give back. It was not only the money that Eddie gave that made a difference, it was Eddie's down to earth presence at the school while talking to the kids about how he grew up and the people who helped him along the way. His presence made an impact on those students. Eddie learned that giving back was important because he, being one of 13 children, knew that helping others would make a difference in someone's life.

Pam Shriver grew up seeing her Mom volunteer at assisted living facilities where many of the residents were incapacitated and often their own children did not even come to visit them. Pam had very close family ties. The whole family including grandparents, aunts and uncles spent time together playing tennis or swimming on the weekends. This laid the groundwork for many open ended discussions around sportsmanship and the need to be gracious when you won and thoughtful when you lost. Pam knew that her talents were special and the truth was her parents never really knew exactly how talented she was until she started beating many of the boys and men on the courts. Her coach had to point out to her parents that letting Pam go pro at the early age of 16 was her path. Pam played for many years then when she retired, she brought a tennis tournament to Baltimore every year for 25 years to raise money for non-profits. Even today, she volunteers and works in the school that her children attend so she can help with fundraising and assisting teachers when they are looking for an extra pair of hands. This is another example of helping your community.

I grew up in a home that supported my entire Brownie and Girl Scout efforts as well as all my sports endeavors throughout junior and senior high school. Growing up in the country on a farm, the summers lent themselves to my Mom creating a 'group summer camp' at the house. The basement became the arts & crafts center and the farm became the nature hut for interesting rocks, leaves, plants and anything else we found outdoors. There were horseback riding opportunities, hiking and biking outings that were great fun. Most of the girls were my age but some were younger. By helping the younger kids, the older kids were given an opportunity to share our experiences as well as learn about each other in a non-school environment. We each had our own activities that we enjoyed more than others did and there was always a give and take attitude while helping others who did not know which side to use when getting up on a horse, or that not all spiders are poisonous, or how to hit a softball or how to play kickball. I had learned as a child that helping others do activities that I was good at, gave me a sense of accomplishment while at the same time helped someone else to learn something new.

Growing up in a very non-Jewish neighborhood was quite different than most of my school friends and I could go riding or be outdoors whenever I wanted. Of course, my Mom felt that being a tomboy was not the most engaging activity for her oldest daughter.

Going to Sunday school for 12 years gave me a very clear understanding of the need to give back to my community. For me that community encompassed all of Baltimore and it was brought to my attention while observing my Mom and my Grandmother who participated in community work throughout the city. My Grandmother (paternal) had become in involved with several Jewish women's group and almost always took a leadership position. My Mom sat on the board of Levindale, the elder care facility that did not discriminate by race or religion for their residents. It was clear to me that I would always feel the urge to give back to my community by volunteering or assisting in raising funds for non-profits.

Having lived in Mexico, it was interesting to me that giving back was not a part of their culture. True in the 1970s Mexico was farther along than other Central or South American countries, but there was no ready-made opportunity to give back to assist others who needed help. Communities had on one side of the street families living in metal or paper shanties and just across the street, there were huge homes with concrete or metal gates with glass on the tops to keep others out.

I had seen poverty during the riots in 1966 in downtown Baltimore and it came as a real shock to me as a teenager. I understood the need to give back to a community needing assistance, but the destruction that took place in the 'ghetto' was horrible. Though Jews and African Americans were equally affected, it was difficult to watch the city government not provide equal assistance to the African America community. Many of the Jewish business owners assisted the African American community more than the local government. It was clear that restoring these communities was equally important to make Baltimore City a better community. The city did come back stronger for both communities, black and Jewish assisted with the creation of a program called the 'Blues' and the organization continued for over 20 years bringing together both communities. The most interesting facet of this program was that it was not about giving charity, it was about restoring trust and understanding in Baltimore City to create a better place to live.

My Mom was quite a strong willed woman who wanted her two daughters to be perfect ladies and it was much harder for me than it was for my younger sister. She loved all the girly things. I did learn to sew, knit and eventually learned needlepoint and crochet. I learned that what was most important to me and my Mom was how to give back to the community. One great thing about my Mom was she never shamed me into doing something that was good for me to do. I was always a leader and giving back was just part of what I had learned from my immediate family.

I was very involved in the youth group at the Synagogue; I would visit Levindale to talk to the elderly who had no family members coming to see them and always volunteered for any activity where I could give assistance to others. I knew that I would always be a giver and not a taker because that was the example that permeated through my family.

A repeated concept throughout this book is finding your passion; however, now is the time to really think about what you can do with your life that will bring happiness, fulfillment, contentment and a real sense of purpose. Your passion is not about work rather it should be about creating that warm and fuzzy spot in your heart and mind that says, "I have made a difference!"

Go to a place that makes your heart radiate with pleasure and know that you have made a difference to someone or to your community at large. You may even need to leave your job or your home while trying to find a job that brings you peace, serenity and happiness. This may seem strange to you at first but as time passes and you become better at what you started to do your self-esteem and self-worth will soar.

We all know that the first step is to get up off the couch and find that non-profit, that volunteer position, find your Big Brother or Big Sister and do something that brings the child out of you, make others feel special and cared for by someone who sincerely cares. In today's world where there is constant strife, war, murders and starvation, one person can make a huge difference in someone else's life. When you make that difference, you will feel really great about having taken that step out the door of your home. The look on a child's face that says you have given something they never had, or the relief in the face of an adult who is learning to read for the first time ever, you will not only see the difference, you will feel the difference you have made to someone in need.

Do you remember when you were a child and your parents wanted you to play ball, swim, read more or perhaps be more caring to others, how that made you feel? Were you ready to jump right in and take the plunge? Probably not. Now as an adult, you can look back and think how those things made you a better person. Perhaps you became captain of your baseball team and every year you won the sportsmanship of the year award. Perhaps you helped several kids in your chemistry class to understand the periodic table of elements so others could get better grades.

These memories might be buried after so many years of struggle and staying afloat in an economy that has still not turned around. Take the time to really think about how you were as a child by helping someone and how much more important that is for so many people struggling. Besides, you might volunteer at a senior day care center and in a few months end up with a job.

The next generation must be engaged in these types of activities and become aware of the need to give back. The rewards that come by doing can only make the feeling all warm and fuzzy.

CHAPTER TWELVE

CREATIVITY ON THE MOVE

The one really great thing I learned living in Mexico is that people are different. Not just from a socio-economic position but in a country like Mexico where there are many people from mixed nationalities and descendants such as the Mayan, Olmec, Aztecs, Mestizos, Criollos and most likely even some Native American, which taught me that everyone is equally important to their country and their community.

Diversity among the baseball players was amazing. Some had college degrees, some never finished high school and some had egos so big their heads barely fit through the door. This diversity also made our jobs more challenging because some of the players were clueless about how to handle money, some were real impulse buyers, some were very religious and some had no values at all but for me, it was all about the client! The great thing about bringing such a diverse group together with such dissimilar ideas, misunderstandings and talent, for me was to be able to make a difference in their everyday lives.

My biggest concern was getting some of the players ready for what happens after baseball. As big of a concern as that was, in the beginning it was teaching them about using a checkbook, understanding the advantages and pit falls of owning or renting a house or an apartment, how many cars they really needed, how important is it for their children to have a good education and how do you invest their money and get them to understand what that means. This was everyday living. What comes after baseball was really more like a snake sneaking up on you and then suddenly, wham – you are facing the rest of your life with no plan! Many of the wives were savvy about life after baseball but for some of the men, retiring was a very scary thought. Some were lucky to become sports casters, others became real estate brokers and some lost all that they had because of drugs or mismanagement of funds.

These things happened because many players do not have many life experiences before become professional athletes. They believed that they would play ball for years and not ever have to worry about life or money after baseball. That is not what really happens. The shock and disappointment about not playing forever is a real obstacle and for some, it is a really hard transition to overcome. Sometimes they have to retire early because their body has just worn itself out, sometimes it is because they are no longer performing at the same level as when they were at age 20 and sometimes, family and other issues take over then before you know it; your career is over.

Every player believes that they are immune to all of these things. Even as they see themselves slowing down, they don't really acknowledge that there is some degree of change in their throwing arm, batting stance, running ability and they chalk it up to just being tired or having an 'off day'. However, after several 'off days', being benched and then not put on the roster for a few weeks, even then it does not really hit home that they are not as strong, not as agile or as fast as they once were. They retain their cockiness and hold onto the belief that their abilities are just the same as they were at 20. Thinking about the future is not an option until you are off the team and not playing. It is a very hard transition and it is necessary to retain confidence and believe in who you are.

Many of the players were from small American towns, leading interesting lives in their community because they had the talent to be a professional athlete. Most of them, upon signing their first contract were making more money than their father had made in his entire lifetime. Few of them really knew how to manage their money and were often living from pay check to pay check. The guys would spend money on foolish things that they believed were giving them stature among their peers but truth be told, it was just the opposite. Many players wanted to buy a car, own a house and buy clothes before they knew if their pay check would cover their monthly expenses. There were players who were more fiscally responsible but most players had that bug to buy and buy. It was interesting to note that if their wife was in town, the financial situation ran slightly more smoothly. With the player being on the road and pay checks delivered to their residences, it was easier for the wife to maintain some control over spending.

Attempting to control the players spending was always a challenge. I can remember getting a call in the middle of the night from a young University of Maryland football player who was in San Diego at a try out for the team. It was about midnight or slightly later when my phone rang and the player, who of course was thinking on West Coast time, just started talking about needing a new suit and wanting to buy something for his wife. Once he slowed down and I told him that they had just enough money to get back to Maryland, there was dead silence and then a barrage of requests, "Could I lend him the money? Could the firm give him an advance? Could he get a loan?" He would do anything to get the money. I listened and then trying not to be condescending or harsh, told him that if he made the team we could talk about his financial situation and asked if he realized, that it was after midnight in Baltimore.

Another more established player who was married, living in both Baltimore and California and already had three cars for two drivers, called me during the off-season. He wanted to buy another car. When I asked, for what purpose, there was no real explanation. I asked him, "There are only two drivers and why would you need four cars?" Needless to say, he waited until he came east and bought another car!

As I learned more about each player and their need to be community oriented by promoting some form of philanthropy, it was often a struggle to get some of them to understand the need to give back.

For some players it was rather difficult to get them to even visit a children's hospital just to sign a few autographs and give a baseball to a sick child. Most of the younger players did not understand that helping others meant giving of themselves to make others feel better.

It was not supposed to be about a monetary reward. What became the most engaging experiences was when some of the more established players who were working with the up and coming players, would often ask them to accompany them to a hospital, a school in the inter-city or to a signing event. This was the beginning of mentorship for these young ball players on the need to give back and how to overcome their discomfort level.

It was clear to me that even though many players came from small towns as local heroes; these young men had little if any understanding of the need to give back. In fact, many of them had a sense of entitlement, really believing they deserved to be paid for any additional events or appearances. At times, I could be very persuasive about their need to attend an event that gave them exposure to the bigger community and how giving back could be an opening for opportunities like TV commercials or other speaking engagements. Being the 'Hatch Lady' often had its benefits.

One of my better characteristics is one of nurturing and caring. Perhaps that came from growing up on a horse farm. By taking care of the animals, horses, dogs, rabbits and stray animals that wandered into our fields this inoculated me with sympathy, empathy and an understanding of the necessity to care about what the animals needed. Also living in a foreign country gave me the ability to give back to others in need. These experiences combined with my upbringing helped me understand that giving back is essential. I wanted to help the players realize the benefits of caring for others less fortunate in our community. In part, some of this entailed teaching players' basic life skills and making them really understand, giving back is a wonderful way to help others. I also realized that their understanding of managing their money was important but not necessarily an easy concept to grasp.

Giving back to the community, to create a better place to live, is often rewarding for some players, while others, are not the least bit receptive. Giving back is not something that everyone wants to embrace. It is part of who I am and who I will always be. I also understood that some ethnicities do not engage in philanthropic opportunities in the same manner in which I was raised. I needed to be very cognizant on how I approached each player as well as know when to step back and let them make their own decisions about giving back. Though giving back is important to me, I realized that I could not force my values on them. The give and take that occurred between the players and me was based on each player's personality and needs.

There were times when a team's general manager would call and ask if I could persuade a player to participate in a particular organization or event for community exposure. Sometimes I was successful and other times not so much.

Creating just the right situation for each player was not always easy. I realized that sometimes, it was easier when I accompanied the player on his first few outings to get a grasp on the situation and what it meant to give back. Often a young player visiting a children's hospital for the first time, would leave with tears in his eyes because the kids were really appreciative of his time and efforts to make them each feel better, if only briefly. It is amazing how some players realized immediately how much joy they bring to these sick children and how other players leave, saying they can't do this again because it is too sad and disconcerting.

Each player is different. One thing I have learned over the years through all of my experiences is that I have to be aware of each individual personality's needs and wants and make life better for each individual. This is why I get up each day knowing that I might be able to help one more person.

Philanthropy takes many forms and I have always encouraged any philanthropic endeavor. For me philanthropy can be as easy as helping someone just starting their career, make the right connections with others, help write a proposal or being a mentor on a regular basis. Since no one is raised with the same values and core beliefs, my attitude has always been, be there for the needs of my clients, players and my friends and assist them in any way that I can.

As a professional fundraiser, the best part of my job is to bring together a non-profit organization and an investor so that both parties walk away with a feeling of win/win. The feeling of goodwill and gratitude from each participating party in the deal makes me ecstatic when I have created a good match. This is what makes a community come alive with an understanding that by helping each other this is a great 'mitzvah' which means it is a real blessing.

In many ways, I could be considered a teacher of sorts, always fighting for the underdog whether it is for a cause or assisting someone else with getting ahead in their career or just in their life. Not everyone reacts with the same graciousness towards my abilities when I attempt to assist them. I am grateful that I am very cognizant when someone is resistant to giving back. However, when I see someone suddenly taking their own initiative and start giving back to the community it means that they understand they are making a better life for everyone in that community. No one is perfect and I have certainly had clients and players along the way, not caring one bit about engaging with a community or wanting to help anyone else. Being a connector and networker has given me; the opportunity to bring people together that otherwise would not have the opportunity to meet.

Over the years, it has been easy to help others because when I look back at my own growth, I was assisted along the way by a variety of mentors, which only enhanced my desire to give back. My resources were strong and though I never really considered that I was the creative type, I always seemed to be able to connect the right people.

Philanthropy to me is about giving financial support, giving assistance to those in need whether it is finding them a job, helping with a project or being there for someone in need. I take that responsibility very seriously. My Dad's advice about being a leader and not a follower has made me a better person. Working with others who want to understand the various opportunities in giving back is a win/win for everyone. The non-profit finds an investor, the investor finds a cause they can promote within their community, a young player can become an icon for sick children and a young graduate from college can find a mentor.

All of this leads back to you, the reader getting up off the couch and understanding what will give you the most joy in your life to help others. You don't have to write a check instead, you can volunteer to help a student read or grasp math better. You can visit a child who is sick at a children's hospital and bring some joy into their life. You can mentor someone who is just starting their career. Any one of these ideas will give you the sense of what makes you want to be a better person.

What is the cause that will make you feel like you are giving back? Who do you want to mentor? Can you help an elderly person with their finances and drive them to their doctor's appointment and be an advocate for them? These are all ways to give back and it let's you know that you are making a difference. Every time you step up to the plate to help someone else, you are helping yourself!

CHAPTER THIRTEEN

EVERYONE IS DIFFERENT

Growing up in the country on a horse farm, gave me the freedom to go outside and be free! That meant climbing trees, chasing the horses, taking care of the rabbits, watching the mastiff puppies as they went from being held in your hand one day and two days later crawling up your legs. I could get on my horse any time and ride any trail I wanted. There was a sense of doing whatever I wanted, whenever I wanted. Having that freedom gave me the courage and the fortitude to try anything and do anything. I believed that I was invisible as many kids think they are, but the fact that my Dad treated my brother and me like young adults also made it easier to take the reins and go.

My father would have liked to have three boys. Instead, he got one son and two girls. My being in the middle at the time did not seem to be fortuitous. I realized later in life, it had been my guiding light and opportunity to become a self-confident woman. Though my Dad never said to me 'be a man', he had me do all the things my brother did and also set an example to my younger sister. That was the hard part. Who wants to come in from the barn, change their pants for a skirt and then do something domestic? Not me, that's for sure. I could do just about everything my brother did, except change the tire on the tractor. I could drive a stick shift as well as he did. Even though I was not as good in math and science, I had good grades. At the tender age of 10 or 11, I had a checking account. Why you might ask? My Dad loved to send away for things from the newspaper or a magazine, I learned to write the letter, write the check, mail it and balance my checking account. Although, I didn't really do a good job at balancing my check book. My brother went to South American when he was 20 and I went to Mexico for the first time when I was 17.

My Dad's main occupation was as an owner of a trucking company. He was a very hard worker, leaving the house around 6 am and often not getting home until after 8 or 9 pm. Sometimes he would go into the office on a Saturday morning and he would take me with him. That is where I learned the value of a dollar and had my first opportunity to learn how a business should be run. One of my Saturday duties was to sort the bill of ladings for each truck. I took a pencil, with the eraser side facing down and flip through each stack and being VERY sure, they were in order. Sometimes, I counted the money in the cash draw. My Dad knew the exact amount so, if I was off even by a penny, I had to count it again until it was exact.

The expectation that was created by listening and watching my Dad and my brother, was that I learned a work ethic that was more male than female. I say that because I thought using 'womanly wiles' was foolish and unnecessary. I certainly played better with boys than girls. As I got older, I grew more confident that I could do anything that I wanted to do. For me there was freedom to try anything.

I also realized that so much of what I learned had been through osmosis. I realized that my Dad was a leader in the community and that being a leader was more important than being a follower. I have always taken on leadership roles and at the same time, felt that mentoring and coaching others was a gift. I learned a great deal from my Dad and was quite sad when I lost him when I was only 18.

So, as I have mentioned, my first occupation was as a sports agent. It was a great job and was the best way to learn how to start a business from the ground up. I also learned how to do just about every job there was in the organization except making financial decisions for the players.

I believed I had found my cause in life and I would be there forever. Well, forever was cut short. My colleague and partner just came in one day and told me it was time for me to move on! Was I shocked, yes, but I was also angry and hurt when I found out the reason was financial. This was the first time I felt discrimination for being a businesswoman. Honestly, after I had earned two masters degrees and one in Administrative Sciences I was shocked. I had all the same degrees as the men that I worked with.

It took me some time to get over the disappointment but I moved on and I was able to retain one player who really trusted me. It was very rewarding for me to remain working with that player and made it easier to move on. In the beginning, I felt betrayed and angry that I had worked to grow the business and now I was out the door with no more than, what felt like a kick in the butt. Having good contacts in Baltimore, gave me the opportunity to try something very different from the sports business. I went to work for an advertising agency as a Vice President of the New Business section.

However, I had started doing volunteer work in the community while working and going to graduate school. Fortunately or unfortunately having a family who has been in Baltimore for seven generations it was not too difficult to find an organization that wanted me on their board. I soon realized that it was my name that was more important than what I could do.

I had been gone from Baltimore for almost 10 years going through college and living in Mexico. When I came back, my connections were not terribly strong and I was known as Hya's or Lloyd's daughter. It took a very long time to create my own identity. Once my Mom was grocery shopping, a young woman walked up to her, and said, "Are you Lyn Watner's mother?" Finally, I was vindicated!

I volunteered at the Baltimore Museum of Art, at the Baltimore Symphony, was President of the Board for an organization called the Sexual Assault Recovery Center and in the past few years have been President of my synagogue, condo and on the board of Child First Authority, a non-profit that provides after school programs.

I did get slightly burned out and even took off a year or two from working on boards where I always did the fundraising. Soon, I realized that I really liked fundraising and finally decided that it was time to go out on my own and become my own boss.

I have been working for myself since March of 2013 and have had a variety of clients as well as doing pro bono work for several smaller and start up non-profits. I realized that fundraising is my calling and for me extremely rewarding. What makes it so rewarding, is that I get to bring a prospect and an organization together to create a gift to assist the organization and the investor who will ultimately become involved.

What really kept me engaged with fundraising were all the wonderful relationships I developed over the years. Fundraising and philanthropy are really about building relationships that last for many years. I have held many different positions over the years yet, it is the relationships I built in Baltimore and across the country with investors, who I became friends with that, I mostly value and who are rewarding. I have also had many staff follow me from job to job.

I think that my mentoring became important because I wanted to help staff move up the ladder whenever possible. Listening is the most important characteristic of being a fundraiser. When you ask one question that answer can give you a wealth of information about the prospect. Being engaged with the investor is the most rewarding part of the job. Even today as a consultant, I look for clients that I want to be engaged with for a long time.

Maintaining these relationships over the course of years has been a blessing. For me it has been important to maintain these relationships, to become a better connector for friends, people I meet for the first time and just help people who don't know how to get started in business, in writing their CV or just need some guidance. Giving back in any capacity is rewarding and it becomes even more so when the results provide evidence that the person you helped has made progress.

I realize that I have become the woman that my Dad would have been proud of. I have more friends, contacts and relationships than what I ever believed I would have accumulated over the years. Many of my contacts are not even in Baltimore and it doesn't matter.

I enjoy helping people find themselves or become more productive in their jobs or even young people who are just getting started. Helping others is what I have always done best from the athletes to my friends and even with people, I meet on planes, trains and buses! I learned from my Mother and Grandmother that if you can talk, you not only get directions, you can ask questions galore and find everything about almost anyone when they feel engaged and comfortable. I really feel grateful that I am not afraid to be who I really am and how I do things.

What does this mean for you? It means that you need to dig deep, know who you are and what your passion is! Your passion is what motivates you to get up off that couch. You need to know what is really important to you, so that you can carve out a certain amount of time to help others. By doing this you will have personal satisfaction but not necessarily a financial reward. Do it, because in helping others you not only nourish yourself, you nourish others with hope and expectations they may not have thought possible. There is an indirect pleasure when you become a part of a life that you helped. With that first step to seek out your passion, to make someone else's life better, you suddenly realize that this is what you need to complete your life.

It is important that you love your choices. If you try, too many different things you will most likely burn out and stop doing good. I know that between volunteering and fundraising for non-profits the experience can be draining and sometimes there will be a need to pull back, slow down and take time for yourself. It's more important to find what really gives you pleasure. There are many places where help is needed. Look through the newspaper and go through local magazines. If the city has a neighborhood newspaper or a local paper, mostly likely these publications will have some notification calling for volunteers. Remember that the library is a great vehicle for finding non-profits in need. Everyone has love in their heart that speaks to them that helping someone in need is an incredible contribution to the community. The passion that you feel is the one thing that you can give back to a selfless endeavor. You can make your community a better place.

The first thing you need to do is get up off that couch. Secondly, find the one thing that you feel passionate about. The final step is find out what organization needs volunteers.

When you spend time that benefits others, it gives you personal pleasure. There may not be any financial remuneration, however the personal satisfaction out weighs everything else. What it comes down to is that you are helping someone else directly by enabling them to realize that you have become a part of their life. The gratitude that you feel when you leave your volunteer position and the satisfaction that you feel in your heart, makes a huge difference in your life and how you will live it moving forward.

CHAPTER FOURTEEN

VALUES AND MORALS

I have been fundraising for over 25 years starting when I returned in 1977 after living in Mexico for six years. I had a good life as a child and knew that giving back to my community was important. I didn't start thinking that I would eventually be a professional fundraiser, it just sort of happened.

My first 'ask' was an annual appeal letter for an organization, The Sexual Assault Recovery Center and we raised about $2,000. When I became President of the Board, I started going out and asking corporations for donations. This was my first experience making a 'direct ask' for money. I learned very quickly that sexual assault was not a very popular topic and I was told, "NO!" more times than I wished to count.

The trick is not to take the "NO," as a personal affront. I believed in the cause and knew that at some point I would get a, "Yes," to my request. After getting my first "Yes," I just knew that I was going to like fundraising. What I have always liked the most about fundraising is bringing a prospect or an investor together with the institution. Creating that synergy has always been a rush for me and it feels great to have each party walk away feeling they have made a difference.

I enjoy meeting people and over the years, I have developed a very interesting group of investors that I can engage with and have assisted them in learning about a non-profit they may not know exists. This is the beauty of building strong relationships and maintaining contacts over the years and I have a nack about creative giving and learning about new non-profits. Though I am a native to Baltimore, I have been fortunate to travel for several of the organizations where I worked, giving me the opportunity to build relationships outside of my initial sphere of influence. There is a sense of gratitude for me, knowing that I have maintained the relationships that often come in very handy. Besides fundraising, I am also a good connector of introducing people to each other who need assistance and I find it very rewarding.

The trick to being a 'Great' fundraiser is being a 'Great' listener. Everyone has a story or a need to tell you their story. When you get past the small talk and you have told them your story, it is amazing what a prospect is willing to share. Being a good listener means exactly that and taking notes is rather tacky. So if your mind wanders, think of some tools you can use that will give you a clue as to how to remember what the prospect told you.

Try to create a short hand method that will help you listen and hear what is being said. The prospect wants to feel secure and comfortable that you are not only listening, you are really hearing what is being communicated to you. Building a lasting relationship depends on how you are perceived at the first meeting. Send a follow up note – on any pertinent information that the prospect requested from you, within the next 24 hours. Then, sit down and type out your notes, this is extremely valuable and add those notes after each successive meeting.

Here is a really great, "Aha!" moment when trying to close a big 'ask'. Hopkins was in their first major campaign and part of that campaign included building a new athletic center. At a reunion, I met Ralph, a Hopkins alum who hailed from Houston and was extremely engaged with lacrosse as well as collecting Blue Jay memorabilia, which happens to be the Johns Hopkins mascot. I had other donors I visited in Houston and added Ralph to my list of prospects. I am sure I visited Ralph as many as six or nine times and every time, he took to the men's club for lunch. At the last visit, we ended up in his office where he had a 30-foot long wall, with every type of Blue Jay you could imagine, wood, ceramic, paper mache, paintings, metal and so on and so forth. I was sitting on the sofa facing the collection and Ralph was complaining that his kids were not the least bit interested in the collection and he was concerned what would happen when he was no longer here. I have to say that literally a light bulb went off in my head because we were trying to find a prospect for the new athletic center. Though I had not discussed this with my colleague, I knew exactly what I was going to do.

I said to Ralph, "We are building a new athletic center, how about whenever you are ready we put your collection in the lobby of the new athletic center and we will name the building after you?" Ralph asked what that would cost. I said, "$3 million." And he said, "OK!!!"

My first reaction was GREAT! The second was I should have asked for $5 million. This happened in 1999 and $3 million was a very good 'ask'. I was able to pull all this together because I had listened to Ralph over the past 6 - 7 months when I visited him. I knew what was important to him and what pushed his buttons. It was real clear that he would not have given to a science or writing program when he loved lacrosse. He also had such an incredible affection for his Blue Jay collection and I knew the collection might just be the hook to close the deal. Sure enough it was. Of course, I had not asked my colleague if this was acceptable, I just went ahead and did it. This could have come back to bite me, but I was confident that our Dean of the School of Arts & Sciences and the Associate Dean would be excited and they were. By giving the investor the opportunity to do something wonderful for the university that gave him a leg up in his education which, led to a great job, was the best win/win for Ralph.

I have another story regarding the wife of a Hopkins doctor. Mary's husband was an alum of the Arts & Sciences and was trained at Johns Hopkins School of Medicine. She was not an alum but had become very attached to the group of doctors and spouses that became her community while her husband was alive and even after he passed away. Mary also lived in Houston and I visited her only twice.

The second visit was to make an 'ask' to start a scholarship in her husband's memory. We chatted for quite a while and just as I was about to ask her for a $25,000 gift, she said, "I have a check for you for $250,000." I was so glad, I had not made the 'ask'! This does not happen very often, but when it does, as a fundraiser I thank myself for being alert and a good listener.

The fact that Mary offered a gift that was 10 times what I would have asked for was wonderful and surprising. It was surprising because most of her contact had been through the medical school, but she gave the scholarship for the students in the School of Arts & Sciences. When I asked her, why A & S, she felt that the undergraduate needed more scholarship money than the doctors.

I had the reverse happen one time when an investor had paid off his first $500,000 gift and my colleague sent me out to Colorado Springs to ask him for another $500 k. When I got around to make the 'ask' for $500 k, the elderly gentleman turned red, started choking and I was sure he was going to die. When he finally caught his breathe, he indicated he would only give $50,000. All any fundraiser can do is make their most educated guest what the prospect or investor will give. Whatever the figure, be gracious and thank them profusely!

I have always been a people person and I realize that is partially from how I grew up. My father thought children should be little adults and because we lived on a farm, we did not have regular playmates. So, my brother and I spent more time with adults than with kids our own age. For me it was a great way to grow up because I was able to be a listener and rarely a participant.

Nuances, language and hand gestures were a part of what I learned while listening to the 'old folks' while they talked, bragged and embellished their stories. Time spent with adults gave me a great education about how to listen, learn and know what is really important in building relationships.

Whatever organization I was working for over the years, I built relationships that lasted and were significant in moving my career forward. Each person was an individual that was important to me, not only in that moment but also, at any time, they needed me. I had a notebook of names, addresses, phone numbers, birthdays and anniversaries, children's names and schools they attended and every week I rotated who I was going to call and what else could I learn about them. At times, I would have as many as 150 prospects plus investors in the range of 200. When I called and there was no answer,

I always left a voice mail message! Many of my investors followed me to different nonprofits. Why? Their theory was I would take a position where I believed in the mission and the outcomes of the organization. Staying connected with my investors was natural and actually fun.

I realized that connecting with prospects and investors is not an easy concept for many fundraisers. Why? Many did not want to tell their own story or reveal some personal information that might be inappropriate or they just didn't really like that investor.

Some fundraisers could really connect with the prospect or investor but could not make the 'ask'. Learning to close the 'ask' is essential in this business as is listening, learning and staying connected. The thought of being rejected is huge for many fundraisers. Many times someone could not make the 'ask' because they were talking too much or had not prepared enough to know how much to 'ask' for. I often took newbie fundraisers with me on visits to give them the sense of when to listen, when to talk and when to make the 'ask'. Often upon leaving those visits, they would ask how do I know when the right time is or know when to stop talking.

If you watch body language, posture or even eye movement, you should begin to have idea if you are talking too much, boring them, or talking the right amount of time. Paying attention and watching body language is always a great start to getting to know your client. You should also, keep in mind, it is better to end the conversation and try again another day when your prospect won't look directly at you, or they fidget while you are explaining the organization's mission and vision. This body language may mean that you have lost their attention and you may not be able to hold their attention again. It is not so hard to create a win/win situation if you know your prospect. Everyone is looking for a winner and it can be you. As you feel more confident that you are making progress with every visit and every engagement, one day you will wake up and say I am ready to make the 'ask'. I am not afraid when I'm told, "Thanks but, no." Often an investor or prospect will come back to you three, six or 12 months later and say, "YES!" Then you have made the win/win for everyone.

Meeting people, learning about their lives, finding out what engages them, what they live for and what they like to do can be so appealing and enticing, it becomes part of your life. It's a journey every time you meet someone new. Some will become friends, some will be standoffish and yet they too become givers and along the way, you learn about who you are. It is a great way to turn your own life around, learn about others and how you might want to live your life someday. It's great to have new friends who may be connectors that can make your life better.

CHAPTER FIFTEEN

WHY DO I GET UP EVERY DAY?

Did I just wake up one morning and realize that I had been working for over 38 years, of which 25 years plus were as a professional fundraiser?

Where did the time go and how did I even get to this point? I started out thinking that I would get married, teach and have children. That scenario disappeared quickly. I did however, teach kindergarten when I lived in Mexico and loved every moment. The only problem I had, was that I had favorite students. I realize now that because I did not have a firm concept of a career path, I was able to create my own destiny. It happened by being in the right place at the right time when I became a sports agent.

Even back then, I started talking to non-profits to determine where I might be most effective in their organization. It is amazing how time does just fly by and now I have my own consulting firm working with non-profits. I never really had given any thought to a career path; I knew that giving back to my community was essential for my own wellbeing as well as having had great role models in my Mother and Grandmother. I guess the apple never really does fall far from the tree.

From the very first time that I made an 'ask', I loved fundraising. I realized that if I could ask for $50, I could ask for $500 million; it is just a number. I also realized that I was not ever personally rejected, the prospect either did not like the cause or the mission or felt that the 'ask' was more than the prospect wanted to contribute.

I recognize the creation of a relationship that could last a lifetime. I respect the fact that many of my investors trusted my judgment enough to ask me for advice about their contributions to other non-profits. The most rewarding part of fundraising for me has always been the win/win by bringing the prospect and the organization together generating a contribution that was acceptable to both parties. By engaging a prospect to become an investor, it also gives me the opportunity to build a relationship that helps the investor become more involved with the organization. In fundraising, it is not just about the money, it also about crafting a strategy that allows the investor to become more enmeshed in the mission. An investor may even be given the opportunity to be a board member or an ambassador. In many ways, fundraising for me is like a jigsaw puzzle. It requires me to build a relationship that allows the investor to take advantage of all that the organization can offer.

When I lived in Mexico during the 70s, it was still considered a 'third world' country by many standards. It clearly taught me even more about the need to give back to a community. When I left Mexico, I had no inkling if, I would even have a career path yet, I understood that I had obtained new talents that might be useful. When I became a sports agent, I was just at the right place at the right time and the best part was, I got to use my Spanish for the next 10 years.

I also acknowledged that I loved working and helping others. A huge part of my job as a sports agent was to ensure an atmosphere of trust and understanding that gave an athlete peace of mind and that anything they needed would get done. For me that was the whole concept of giving back to a community where my family had lived for seven generations, I quickly surmised that being a volunteer for any organization would be a great experience.

Having watched my Mother and Grandmother participate in various organizations in Baltimore, I knew that the apple on the tree would always be a nurturing and caring woman. Helping others was imprinted on me at an early age.

My Dad had very definite and finite ideas about how a business should be conducted. When he took me to his office on a Saturday morning, I would get an ear full about how to be tough, honest and unforgiving about any manner of mistrust. Those concepts became the pillars of how I would act as a colleague and businesswoman.

I had already been affected by incidents of discrimination as a sports agent. Being the only woman agent in professional baseball, led to some unpleasant events yet nothing that would have changed my mind about being an agent. Working at the Johns Hopkins Krieger School of Arts & Science as the Director of Development, I presented a very different set of perceptions on how I did business. Though I considered myself quite feminine, I was raised with more male business attributes than most other women.

My business approach was aggressive and assertive for a woman in her early 30s. I had a very strong sense of right and wrong, which did not allow for a great deal of gray when making decisions. I knew I was difficult at times when working with other departments at Hopkins, but I always got the job done. What surprised me the most when I took the position was this was the second time in my career where I was being the bad cop and my supervisor was the good cop.

This was also the case when I was a sports agent. For whatever reason, this conduct often got me in trouble and yet, I was one of the top fundraisers in my department. When Hopkins started their first real campaign to raise $600 million dollars, I was in charge of the hiring for our department. We had started with 4.5 staff at the announcement of the campaign and within the first 18 months, we grew in size to be almost 25 staff members. Many of the new employees were not seasoned fundraisers and they needed a great deal of mentoring, massaging and training before going out in the field. I have always enjoyed helping others so, becoming a mentor and confident was a very rewarding situation for me.

My early perception of relationships between women and men was that women accommodated the men whether they were husbands or their supervisors. As I matured over the years, I realized that was not the norm in most relationships, I began to lighten up and my demeanor took on some new characteristics. I was softer, less aggressive but still assertive when needed and less likely to intimidate others who had gone behind my back. The reality was they knew they should have talked to me before calling one of my investors.

As I began to build relationships, I realized that listening was the most important factor when trying to engage a new prospect. One question could produce an onslaught of pertinent information for me that builds the relationship or cultivates a strategy. The concept of listening in any job is what can make or break a deal and it is fundamental to building a relationship. I found that with new employees, they often asked to come with me on a prospect visit to learn some of my techniques. I was always glad to say yes as long as the prospect did not object to an extra person. Building lasting relationships was so rewarding as well as profitable for the non-profit and the investor.

When more investors followed me from one organization to another, I realized that I had changed so much for the better. The relationships that I built and maintained were not just, because I knew they had money. I built them with the idea that building a strong foundation with an investor becomes an important part of who I had become.

I had always been a nurturer of the animals we had while growing up or with my classmates who needed help in a specific class. What I understand now is that those masculine traits my father so gallantly made me believe in, did not represent the characteristics that were inside of me. To please my father at the time was more important than being who I really was. So as I matured, the softer side, the nurturer and caregiver side of me became stronger. This awakening helped me build even healthier relationships not only with investors and friends, with others who needed a hand.

Now thirty years later, my softer side has taken over and I do a great deal of 'assistance giving'. I have many friends that want to get their children to become a sports agent, or become a career fundraiser, or they ask me to help them figure what is the next step in their career or even how to change careers. I am always willing to help those who feel lost; although in reality, they may only need a more objective perspective. I have colleagues who want help in finding a new job and I am always ready with a list of internet sites that are the best for finding jobs.

When I started my consulting business, I took two coaching classes with a group of entrepreneurial women. I got a call from one of the women asking if I could help Nancy make inroads into the

Major League Baseball Association. Of course, I called Nancy and it turned out she wanted to present a proposal to the Association to coach retired baseball players on how to figure out what they wanted to do with the rest of their lives. We worked together and determined that the best course of action was to find the top ranking woman on staff that might be interested in just such a program. After a few calls to the Association, Nancy found the right person to talk to. Once the proposal was presentable, it was delivered and the response given was that it might be more than the players could afford. Nancy is still attempting to adjust her proposal with the understanding this was her first attempt at trying something on her own and it may not become a reality. I have done a great deal of coaching and mentoring over the years and I have found it to be a great way to meet interesting people as well as being able to give them ideas they may or may not implement. At the very least, they gained knowledge that can be used in the future.

Having lived in a Spanish speaking foreign country, it was natural to use that skill as our sports business grew with more players arriving from countries in Central and South America. It was natural that those players would turn to me for advice because I could easily explain ideas we thought were worthwhile for them as investments or how to make a purchase they could afford like a car or a house. I was still the 'gringa', the pale faced American to many of these players yet they knew I was invaluable in helping them keep their lives on track. Unlike Eddie Murray, the Latin players trusted me almost immediately because I spoke their language. When I first returned to Baltimore and before I had a paying job, I translated at the Kennedy Krieger Institute for Latin children with disabilities. It was very rewarding and I really felt like I was making a difference for these families.

Trust is a very essential part of who I am and in what I do. My word is all I have and even if the deal is sealed with a handshake, the deal still depends on me to carry out the agreement. I have had incidents where a finance officer in a health care facility used money that was supposed to build a future children's center was instead being used for the orthopedic building that was under construction. I felt that my credibility was on the line if the investor ever found out the money was being used for something other than her wishes, I had everything to loose. Integrity and honesty have always been an incredible part of who I am. To build trust with your prospects, investors, non-profits, friends and family, you must be able to truly look someone in the eye and let them know you are trustworthy.

As I have matured over the years with my own consulting firm, it is clear to me that when clients, investors and non-profits work together with honesty and integrity, the outcome is a win/win situation. I've been able to influence both sides of the table and have shown by coming together this brings value to both parties. I think my ability to build good relationships is that I am not afraid to get to know someone from the inside out and I am not afraid to ask anyone for anything. I understand that this fearless trait was passed on to me by each generation in my family.

My maternal Grandmother and Mother could talk to anyone and within 10 or 15 minutes of meeting, a stranger would know that person's story. I used to think it was an invasion of someone's privacy and now I realize it is an essential part of what I do for my work. There are few things in this life that are really free. Really listening is an important skill to become a volunteer in a non-profit or meeting a potential prospect or even a potential date.

Why is this? People want to be who they are and even if it sometimes comes across as puffery, they are trying to let you know exactly who they are. Listening and asking the occasional question, creates a bond that could last a lifetime. Some people really don't like small talk and it can be like pulling teeth to get them to talk. If that is the case, then dig deep in your psyche for a story that might be compelling and show them who you are. You will need to show them the benefit of communicating and becoming more open to revealing who they really are. Occasionally you meet someone who just won't open up. This doesn't always mean they aren't interested it may not be the right time is now.

The more you can make a difference the more satisfaction you will derive from volunteering and getting to know the non-profit that you are working with. Every day that you show up is every day that you learn more about each person. You will be surprised and delighted in how YOU have been able to change someone's doubtful perception to how genuine you are about helping others.

Every community wants to know that their organizations are

making a difference. To show that the organization is making a difference means engaging the entire community through participation and building stronger influences through staff and volunteers. Volunteers know that every day while working with people in need, they are raising the stakes by bettering a community's reputation. It is gratifying for an organization knowing that a volunteer has played a role in making a difference.

Remember you can get up off that coach and change the environment around your block, in the next municipality and in the entire state! Make this your goal and you will soar like an eagle from all the gratitude and good will you have given to others.

EPILOGUE

Life is filled with revelations and dreams that may never have been expected. I would have never have contemplated that I could write a manuscript about the two areas of life I know the most about, sports and philanthropy. Though I came from a family who loved horseracing, football and basketball and parent and grandparents that promoted giving back to their communities, I write because I really believe I had something to say and I know that anyone who truly wants to make a difference can do so with their generosity, with their time and their own spirit. This book is intended to offer guidance in how to make your life fuller by giving your community the gifts you have to give.

I have come to realize that the more you are challenged the better person you become. Each experience will change your heart, your mind, your ego and your authenticity will shine. Giving back is a miracle for you. Become who you knew you always were inside but afraid to let out!

ABOUT THE AUTHOR

Lyn Watner lives in Baltimore, Maryland with Emmie. She graduated from Drew University and lived in Mexico for 6 years.

Lyn was the first woman to be an agent in Major League Baseball from 1976-1986. She has been a professional fundraiser for over twenty-five years and in March 2013, she started her own consulting firm, LMW Non Profit Associates.